RECEIVING THE WORD OF GOD

THE ANNUAL BISHOP OF NEW YORK BOOKS

RECEIVING
THE WORD OF GOD

By

ROBERT E. TERWILLIGER

Ph.D., S.T.M.
Rector of Christ Church
Poughkeepsie, New York

Foreword by
HORACE W. B. DONEGAN
Bishop of New York

MOREHOUSE-BARLOW CO.
New York
1960

139713 © 1960 by Morehouse-Barlow Co.
Library of Congress Catalog Card No. 60-6115

The Scripture quotations in this book marked "RSV" are
from the Revised Standard Version of *The Holy Bible*, copy-
righted 1946, 1952, and 1957 by the Division of Christian Education, National Council of the Churches of Christ in the United
States of America.

PRINTED IN THE UNITED STATES OF AMERICA
BY THE HADDON CRAFTSMEN, INC., SCRANTON, PA.

TO

the memory of
ELMER JAY COOK

Priest, Professor,
Preacher of the Word of God

FOREWORD

IS THERE a word from the Lord?" This question is as old as man, and as new as the morning. To answer this question in the negative, or not to answer this question at all, is to live in uncertainty, if not in despair. This book, which I have chosen as the Bishop of New York Book for 1960, is written out of the firm conviction that the answer to this question is an affirmative one: "Receiving the Word of God is the most important experience in life."

The Church is taught in the Prayer Book to pray that the ministers of God may have grace to set forth God's "true and lively Word," and that the people of God may have grace to "hear and receive" His holy Word. Many books are written from the perspective of the one who proclaims the Word of God. Few books come to mind which are written from the perspective of the one who receives the Word of God.

7

The doctrine of the Word of God is as old as the Church. This book sets forth this doctrine in all of its manifold richness. Its central affirmation is that Jesus is the Word of God, the "true Light which lighteth every man that cometh into the world." It is unique in endeavoring to answer the question of how the Word of God may be more effectively received through the Bible, the liturgy, preaching, and in the everyday life of the Christian. Its concern is deeply pastoral and reflects the wide experience of a faithful shepherd of souls.

It is my earnest hope that this book may be widely read and studied in the Church, for its message "truly received" contains within it the promise of the renewal both of the life of the Christian and the Church.

HORACE W. B. DONEGAN
Bishop of New York

PREFACE

THIS book is written for a practical purpose. It is intended to make the encounter between the Word of God and the reader happen more effectively.

Most writings on this subject have dealt with the proclamation of the Word, and that chiefly in the Bible and preaching. This book takes another perspective. It is conceived from the standpoint of the receiver. Furthermore, it seeks to recognize the meaning of the Word in its New Testament fullness, showing how it can be found in greater completeness in a liturgical tradition.

If these pages are in any way useful, the fact may be largely attributed to the education given the writer by his parish, Christ Church, Poughkeepsie, during his past ten years as rector.

ROBERT E. TERWILLIGER

CONTENTS

CHAPTER I

JESUS THE WORD OF GOD

JESUS CHRIST is the Word of God!

This is the Christian certainty. In our time, being sure of anything is a rare occurrence. The possession of assurance is now as ever one of the distinctive marks of a Christian. From the first days of the Church the disciples of Jesus have held the astonishing conviction that in Him God actually communicated with men. They have been sure that through Him God made Himself known, and revealed the meaning of existence.

A sense of meaninglessness is growing in our society. This is at once painful and dangerous. It is painful because the source of the mental problems of many people now is an uncertainty which leads to a feeling of uselessness. It is dangerous because the development of new powers and possibilities for the human race through science has made it imperative that we know what we are doing. The chance of disaster grows with the lack of a sense of direction. This applies not only to the danger of war, but also to the destruction of the human mind that can come through new devices for its manipulation.

How frequently the question is asked before a modern painting, "What does it mean?" Faced by the distortion, abstraction, apparent confusion, someone remarks with exasperation, "A child could do it." There have even been "experiments" to show that apes can paint in modern style. This approach reveals a sad lack of understanding. The world of modern art is not a child's world nor an ape's world. Naturally there are charlatans among artists as there are elsewhere. The poor draughtsman and the foolish man can perpetrate a fraud and call it an abstraction. It is a demonstrable fact, however, that the contemporary artists such as Picasso, Rouault, and Braque changed their style from an earlier realism. They did not choose the techniques for which they became famous or infamous because they could not draw. They developed styles whose purpose was not so much to create beauty as to interpret reality as they saw it. Frequently their work contains profound psychological symbolism that former artists could not attain because of their naturalism. The torment of their work is a mirror of the modern mind. It is one of the functions of art to interpret a culture. They paint a fractured world because that is the way they have come to see it. There is something prophetic in the way they portray the agony of the human spirit in a society from which the certainties are passing.

The causes for this unsureness are manifold. Clearly, it is in part the result of the shock of two terrible wars and the experience of economic insecurity in recent decades. But men have experienced violent tragedy and poverty before. Sometimes such eras have been moments of great faith. Surely the problem is deeper than just historical. Something has happened to the human spirit. We have ceased to affirm the moral, intellectual, and religious certainties our fathers possessed. Sometimes we wistfully long for the confidence of other days. We symbolize this nostalgia by reviving past styles in art and fashions in clothes. We may cherish the antique, but we cannot return. This is the age to which we belong, and in which we must live. Therefore we must seek to understand what has happened to us.

One reason for our uncertainty is materialism. In its many forms it appeals to our age because it seems to give something concrete to rely on. We can be sure of what we see and hear, of what we possess and manipulate.

There are several sorts of materialism. There is the sophisticated kind which we may call "scientism." This is the belief that the only possible answer to the meaning of things is to be found in science. It is notable that many eminent scientists have departed from this position, if they ever held it. More destructive than the materialism of scientists is the popular notion of what scientists are supposed to think. The layman in this field may feel that scientists all believe that only matter exists, and because of the great authority of their scientific achievement, he loses a sense of the reality of spiritual things.

It may be, however, that the most damaging kind of materialism is a by-product of science. Because of the truly fantastic conquest of the natural world, we are now capable of enjoying material blessings which are so impressive that they may occupy our lives altogether. This is a crude kind of materialism which many peoples of the world come to identify with the American way. We are despised because we are so terribly distracted by the things of the world that we give no time to our souls and to the things of eternity. This is not the picture which we have of ourselves, but it is the caricature which is made too consistently to be ignored. It is no new thing, but the old human foolishness portrayed by Jesus in the man who on the night of his death was occupied with plans for building warehouses for his possessions. It is this practical

materialism, rather than the intellectual materialism of
the scientist, which blinds so many millions to the
reality of spiritual things.

Perhaps even more effective than sheer materialism
in dissolving our convictions has been the appearance
of "psychologism." It may well be that the greatest
scientific advance of our time will prove to be in the
realm of the human mind. There has been much suspicion of psychology and its application on the part of
religious men. Some of this has been amply justified.
However, it cannot be questioned that there has been
a real discovery of truth in psychiatry and psycho-
analysis. The problem arises when the sense of spiritual reality is dissolved because everything is explained
away solely in terms of psychological origin. This
mistake has deprived many a man of his faith when
he was in the hands of an unwise practitioner. Again
it can be said that the greater problem is not what
psychologists believe, but what it is popularly supposed they believe. The jargon of this science has
become part of the vocabulary of the ordinary man.
In periodicals, newspapers, and television he hears of
complexes, neuroses, psychoses, and the rest. He may
become deeply suspicious of his own convictions because he fears they may be only the deliverance of his
childhood, his glands, or his long-forgotten emotional
shocks.

In reaction to these attitudes many people have turned to religion, somehow feeling that there must be some truth there. However, this return has been marked by a lack of conviction. There is indeed curiosity about religion but an unusual lack of corresponding growth in commitment. How many people remark that they are "interested in all religions"! There is a religious relativism and a corresponding moral relativism which leads to the opinion that there is no possible way of deciding what is true or false, what is right or wrong. All of this is further complicated by the contemporary passion for toleration. Naturally the evils of religious prejudice, bigotry, and persecution are repulsive. In the interest of proper religious freedom, however, some have apparently come to fear such things so greatly that they are suspicious of any kind of religious certainty. The "true believer" is considered a dangerous man.

The result of all of this has been the development of religious indecisiveness. What you and I believe is supposed to depend upon our circumstances. What is true for you may not be true for me. Consequently we may lose the sense of truth altogether. We may be very much interested in religion as an esthetic or emotional experience, but not as an intellectual or moral one.

A symbol of this state of mind may be found in the meditation room in the United Nations, where the decorations and appointments are deliberately designed to mean nothing definite so that men of all convictions may use it equally.

In the midst of our spiritual insecurity surely we must ask again the old prophetic question "Is there a word from the Lord for us?"

It is the joy of the Christian to proclaim that there is. He believes that there is a God-given answer to the ultimate questions of human life. It is important, however, to understand what sort of answer it is. It is not a theoretical one in the sense that it is the result of speculation and logical thinking. He believes that the answer to the ultimate questions has come to him, not that he has discovered it through his own cleverness. He can declare that the present sense of meaninglessness can be dissolved by the Word of God. This is a very profound affirmation. To understand its meaning, we must return to its use in the Scriptures. In fact, it is the proper task of the Church at this time to recover the doctrine of the Word of God in its fullness.

When the ordinary Christian hears the phrase "Word of God," he doubtless thinks of the Bible, or perhaps of sermons. In the back of his mind there may lurk some memory of the prologue to the Gospel according to St. John, the beautiful passage which he did not quite comprehend when it was read in church at Christmas. He should not be blamed for this inadequate impression. For centuries, particularly since the Reformation, the impression has been given that the Word of God is essentially verbal. Those who have been most concerned to maintain its centrality have been exponents of traditions which emphasize the Scriptures and preaching, sometimes at the expense of the sacraments. Those of more Catholic tendency, who could have amplified the teaching, have largely left the use of the term to their opponents. It is particularly unfortunate that Christians of the West are so unfamiliar with the thought and devotion of Christians of the East in the Orthodox Churches whose ethos is so permeated with the awareness of the Word of God as the early Christians knew it. After all, it was in the East that the idea originated.

In the New Testament the Word of God is a dynamic idea. St. Paul frequently uses the term in a way which indicates that it is the very presence of the power of God. For instance, he writes in his First Epistle to the Thessalonians:

> And we also thank God constantly for this, that when you received the word of God which you heard from us, you accepted it not as the word of men but

as what it really is, the word of God, which is at work in you believers.

—*I Thessalonians 2:13 RSV*

Somewhat later the writer of the Epistle to the Hebrews has an even stronger and more developed conception:

For the word of God is living and active, sharper than any two-edged sword, piercing to the division of soul and spirit, of joints and marrow, and discerning the thoughts and intentions of the heart. And before him no creature is hidden, but all are open and laid bare to the eyes of him with whom we have to do.

—*Hebrews 4:12-13 RSV*

A change has occurred: the Word of God is thought of as personal. It is no longer "It," but "He." It is none other than Jesus Christ.

Again in the strange imagery of the Revelation of St. John the Divine we encounter the Word as the figure of the horseman on the Day of Judgment, representing Jesus Christ triumphant:

Then I saw heaven opened, and behold, a white horse! He who sat upon it is called Faithful and True, and in righteousness he judges and makes war. His eyes are like a flame of fire, and on his head are many diadems; and he has a name inscribed which no one knows but himself. He is clad in a robe dipped in blood, and the name by which he is called is The Word of God.

—*Revelation 19:11-13 RSV*

Finally we find the fullest declaration of the meaning of the Word of God in the beginning of the Fourth Gospel. This has always been recognized as one of the greatest sections of the New Testament, even by men who did not understand it. In fact, during the Middle Ages it was recited superstitiously as a charm to invoke divine power. Its beauty of expression as well as its profundity reach us even in translation.

> In the beginning was the Word,
> And the Word was with God,
> And the Word was God.
> The same was in the beginning with God.
> All things were made by him;
> And without him was not any thing made that was made.
> In him was life;
> And the life was the light of men.
> And the light shineth in darkness;
> And the darkness comprehended it not. . . .
> That was the true Light,
> Which lighteth every man that cometh into the world.
> He was in the world, and the world was made by him,
>   and the world knew him not.
> He came unto his own,
> And his own received him not.
> But as many as received him,
> To them gave he power to become the sons of God,
>   even to them that believe on his name:
> Which were born,
>   not of blood,

nor of the will of the flesh,
nor of the will of man,
but of God.
And the Word was made flesh,
and dwelt among us,
(And we beheld his glory,
the glory as of the only begotten of the Father,)
Full of grace and truth.

—St. John 1:1-14

When the prologue to the Fourth Gospel is read,
it obviously recalls another equally famous passage of
Scripture; namely, the creation story at the beginning
of Genesis. Surely this is no coincidence. See how in
these words the same conception of the creativity of
the Word appears, as God calls the world into being:

In the beginning God created the heaven and the earth.
And the earth was without form, and void;
And darkness was upon the face of the deep.
And the Spirit of God moved upon the face of the
waters.
And God said, let there be light:
and there was light.
And God saw the light,
that it was good. . . .
And God said, let there be a firmament in the midst of
the waters,
and let it divide the waters from the waters. . . .
And God said, let us make man in our image,
after our likeness. . . .

—Genesis 1, passim

As the poem of creation progresses, the phrase "And God said" is reiterated again and again. Obviously this does not mean that God was calling into nothingness to make things emerge. God's speaking is God's action; His Word is His deed. The Word of God is not simply His utterance, it is His creating power. Yet since speaking is intelligible communication, it does signify that God's work has meaning. This is the Hebrew concept of the origin and significance of the world.

Now the Greek also had his special meaning for the Word. In Greek philosophy a *Logos* teaching (*Logos* meaning "Word") had emerged, particularly among the Neo-Platonists. It had many variations, but the essential idea was that reality comes into being by the agency of a rational creative principle. This principle was called the *Logos*. Clearly this is a notion which could be assimilated to the Hebrew concept of creation, and was used by Christians in the Mediterranean world to interpret their Lord. What they actually were saying was that in Jesus He by whom all things were made in the beginning, He who is the rational creative principle, has come into the world to show their meaning. The significance of reality is apparent in Jesus because in Him the One who made the worlds appears in human form. The Greek would not be pleased by the idea of the *Logos* becoming involved in flesh, for to him the flesh was undesirable, and salvation was escape from the body. Yet this affirmation was boldly made because Christians when they became aware of Jesus were constrained to say that in His person the meaning of things comes clear.

What sort of person could evoke this response? What sort of Jesus do we find in the New Testament? What sort of figure could be called the Word of God?

It would be good for the modern American Christian to seek for a while to forget what he thinks he knows about Jesus and to return to the Bible itself in order to see exactly how He is presented. He would make certain discoveries which might surprise him. One of them would surely be how little we really know about Jesus. This is of quite as much importance as what we do know about Him. It must be remembered that what we have in the New Testament was enough to convert the earliest Church, the martyr Church. It was enough to create the Church of the classical world which became the mightiest spiritual power in that declining culture. Yes, it has to be said, what we have in the New Testament is all we know about Jesus' life on earth. Therefore, it is all we need to know about Him.

The New Testament does not give us a real biography of Jesus. From time to time, men have written so-called "Lives of Christ." They have pieced together narratives from the Gospels and have produced very interesting accounts of Jesus. These books have their value, for they show how men have been devoted to their Lord. Frequently the stories are beautiful, but the details have had to be imagined. The materials for a "Life of Christ" are just not available. In the now classic study called *The Riddle of the New Testament*, by the late Sir Edwyn Hoskyns and Noel Davey, these scholars wrote:

> A biography of Jesus cannot be provided. Further, no single incident in His life or fragment of His teaching, if it be isolated from its context and detached, can be rendered intelligible, even if it be judged to be historical. From a mere collection of fragments, selected from the whole tradition and arbitrarily declared authentic, no outline of the concrete figure of Jesus can be drawn which for one moment carries conviction. If such a selective method be adopted, we might picture a religious personality who taught the "brotherhood of men" and the "fatherhood of God"; or we might roughly sketch an ethical system on the basis of a few aphorisms, and suppose that Jesus was a teacher of ethical principles, or we might sketch the career of a reformer of Jewish piety; or we might discover a religious mystic, or disclose a man possessed of intense spiritual insight depending upon a peculiar religious experience; or indeed, by piecing together a different selection of fragments, we might equally well describe the epiphany of

a divine person, who at no point touched human life as we know it. But these would be, not historical reconstructions, but simply selections of what seems to us convenient, or edifying, or useful, or monstrous.[1]

The ordinary Christian who is not a scholar can perceive this about the Gospel according to St. John. It is easy to see that the picture of Jesus there is an interpretation of His meaning rather than a careful account of His life. The Fourth Gospel may actually be the greatest Gospel because it penetrates most profoundly into the mystery of the nature of Christ. Here is a book which is obviously intended to show what Jesus means rather than what Jesus did. The chronology of the events is different from what we find elsewhere. Even the vocabulary of Jesus is changed. This would not disturb the early Christian for whom this work was written. He would understand its purpose and the sort of literature it is. For instance, there is no account of the Last Supper and the institution of the Eucharist. The writer does not trouble to tell that tale again. He assumes it, and in its place presents the cherished discourses on the Bread of Life and the Vine and the Branches, and the high-priestly prayer. This is a moving portrayal of what the living Lord continually does in His Church, but it is not a picture of the historical Jesus.

[1] Edwyn Hoskyns and Noel Davey, *The Riddle of the New Testament* (New York: Harcourt, Brace and Company, 1947), pp. 171-172.

The first three Gospels, commonly called the Synoptics, seem to have more concrete recollections of Jesus. However, they were not written as lives of Christ but as confessions of faith. They contain materials which had been assembled for use in preaching and worship. Even in them, we cannot find many things which the modern man would dearly love to know about Jesus. Nowhere do we have a description of Jesus' appearance. We do not know the shape of His face, the color of His eyes, whether He was tall or short, agile or slow of movement. We do not know what He was doing during most of the years He lived. Indeed, we do not really know when He was born, how many years He lived, or the length of His ministry. In fact, it must be said that faith in Jesus Christ as the Word of God does not rest upon our knowledge of Jesus as a fully-known personality.

There are many men in history about whose lives we know little, who have made their mark because of their teaching. It is not necessary that we should have biographies of Plato, Thomas Aquinas, or Shakespeare in order to know their power. Perhaps Jesus is this sort of person. There have been many who thought so. They have believed in Jesus as the Word because of His words.

Some years ago it was popular to say that the Christian faith should be the religion *of* Jesus rather than the religion *about* Jesus. It was assumed that the early Christianity was a simple following of the ethical precepts of Christ. Here again it is necessary to come to certain negative conclusions. There is, in fact, nothing about Jesus' ethical teaching which is especially unique to Him. Most of it is the reinterpretation of the Old Testament morality in its best moments. Some of it can be readily paralleled in the utterances of other philosophers and religious leaders. One characteristic of Jesus' teaching is often overlooked—its absoluteness. God's law requires *complete* love for Him with heart, mind, soul, and strength and the love of all men, even our enemies. This is stated in the Summary of the Law, articulated classically in the Sermon on the Mount, and forms the burden of Jesus' teaching about the Kingdom of God. If such a demand is made upon men, it could hardly be called Gospel, good news. If this is the Word of God to men, and this alone, then it would lead us to final despair. Who has fulfilled this requirement?

What we know about Jesus shows that strangely His teaching which is impossible for us is fulfilled in Him. This does not necessarily make Him attractive. He stands before us as an ethical example who judges us by the very contrast between His life and ours. The very perfection of His nature makes us cry out for more than this. If He is what man ought to be, only God can make it possible. We need not only an example, we need a saviour! We must not only have His presence; we must have His power!

Jesus declares that He meets this need. The really unique element in His teaching is His conception of Himself. He made it plain that He believed He had an absolutely unique mission. It is doubtless impossible to give a full answer to the question of how He thought of Himself. This is to say the inner consciousness of Christ is not open to our observation. He was a real man, no matter what more we may believe of Him. In all probability He came to the realization of His vocation gradually, just as we do. Surely the Old Testament, particularly the insights of the prophets, guided Him to the awareness of what He must do. He came ultimately to the conviction that upon Him was laid a burden of obedience unto death. To continue His unremitting attack on unrighteousness, to continue this in Jerusalem, the very center of vested hypocrisy and piosity, would be predictably fatal. He did not, however, think of His death as something that was simply going to happen to Him. He considered it as an act which He must accomplish.

Jesus is no passive figure in this drama, but the main actor. There was a necessity which compelled Him that is reflected constantly in His own words about His own destiny. He used the language of His people to make plain that there was a special purpose in His life. He permitted Peter to speak of Him as the Christ, "the Anointed One." He announced His mission in terms of messianic hope. He used apocalyptic language, declaring Himself to be the Son of Man, the final Lord of history. Furthermore, He undertook the prerogatives which belong to God and God's agent. In the presence of His opponents He forgave sin. He dared in His own Name to change the law of God. He even said He was bringing God's reign. What he did publicly in His preaching, He fulfilled privately in the night in which He was betrayed when He made plain that His life was being given for the restoration of the relationship between God and man.

What Jesus taught about Himself inevitably provoked the charges of blasphemy. This is a conception notably absent in the consciousness of modern men. Blasphemy was very terrible to the Jew, for he had been reared in a tradition fraught with a great sense of the holiness of God. The worst thing a man could do was to usurp God's prerogatives, and this the enemies of Jesus accused Him of doing. He was killed not because they did not understand His message, but because they did. His claim about Himself was fatal.

This is the critical question about Jesus—was He right or was He wrong? If He was wrong, then quite obviously He is not to be trusted as an authority in ethical matters. He would be either mad or a charlatan. The decision has to be made on the basis of more than His own claim. What was the ultimate result for Him and for the world? It is here that we have to make up our minds about the Resurrection.

When Jesus was preached in the earliest Christianity, He was first of all proclaimed as the risen and living Lord. The earliest books of the New Testament are the Epistles of St. Paul. They all have one characteristic which may strike the modern Christian as strange; they contain no personal reminiscences of Jesus, nor do they dwell upon His ethical teaching. They focus on Christ's claim to be the Deliverer of mankind. They present Him as God's act. They show Him as the one sent by the Father to do something essential for the salvation of the whole creation. Jesus Christ is the only one who is so radically obedient to God's will that, when this obedience leads to death, that death becomes a sacrifice for sin, and the overthrow of all of the powers of evil which concentrate their full force on Him. Indeed, even death is overcome, and Christ is alive, ever present to the disciple, and, though unseen, already reigning over history.

This is, for instance, summarized in this way by the
Apostle Paul:

> Now I would remind you, brethren, in what terms
> I preached to you the gospel, which you received, in
> which you stand, by which you are saved, if you hold
> it fast—unless you believed in vain.
>
> For I delivered to you as of first importance what I
> also received, that Christ died for our sins in accord-
> ance with the scriptures, that he was buried, that he
> was raised on the third day in accordance with the scrip-
> tures, and that he appeared to Cephas, then to the
> twelve. Then he appeared to more than five hundred
> brethren at one time, most of whom are still alive, though
> some have fallen asleep. Then he appeared to James,
> then to all the apostles. Last of all, as to one untimely
> born, he appeared also to me. For I am the least of the
> apostles, unfit to be called an apostle, because I perse-
> cuted the church of God. But by the grace of God I am
> what I am, and his grace toward me was not in vain.
> On the contrary, I worked harder than any of them,
> though it was not I, but the grace of God which is with
> me. Whether then it was I or they, so we preach and so
> you believed.
>
> *I—Corinthians 15:1-11 RSV*

This is the sort of proclamation which converted
the Mediterranean world of the first century. This is
the sort of figure which evoked the belief that Jesus
is God's revelation to man. It is completely consistent
with Jesus' own understanding of Himself. The notable feature of this message is that Jesus is presented not

as a reminiscence but as a presence. He is proclaimed as the creative Act of God which men encounter in personal experience.

The same fact is true elsewhere in the New Testament. It is declared in many different writings, representing various points of view, moods, and personalities. There is, however, a consistency in the witness borne by all of the records. Whether we read the Epistles of St. Paul, the Synoptic Gospels, or St. John, whether we seek to understand the almost terrifying images of the Apocalypse, we find a real consensus that the importance of Jesus lies in what He was and did. To understand this it is first necessary to perceive the New Testament understanding of the human situation.

The early Christians, indeed most Christians of all centuries, have taken a very realistic view of man. In this they are at one with the Hebrew tradition set forth in the Old Testament. Man is perceived as the creation of God, made in God's image. This does not mean that there is a spark of divinity in each of us. That is an old pagan idea. Man made in the image of God means that he is capable of converse with God, that he can receive God's Word. He has the gift of reflecting God's image, as a mirror receives an image.

However, this original nature is imperfect now. The great myth of the damage of human nature is to be found in the early chapters of Genesis. It is assumed everywhere in the New Testament. Naturally, the story is not historical, in the sense that it accurately reports a single very early event. It is, rather, biographical. The tale of Adam and Eve is the story of every human life. Perhaps it can be expressed in terms of conscience. There is within all of us a conflict between what we may call the "is" and the "ought." We are aware of what we should do, of the good which should be the goal of our choices. Yet we must be sad as we reflect upon the course of our life. It is like the awareness of a lost paradise. The "ought" is our Garden of Eden. The "is," the actual reality, is our exile. This does not mean that man is totally depraved, but that all of our decisions are imperfect. This is the cause of that condition which we call sin.

Sin is a religious concept. It is frequently misunderstood because it is assumed to be simply a moral one; that is, the violation of a code of ethics. Sin is a relationship which we sustain toward God because we keep ruining the nature which He gave us by the misuse of our freedom. In the Bible, it is understood to be a lostness, a loneliness, an alienation, which has in it a sense of contamination. Furthermore, this state is a powerful one, working disastrous results in human life which emerge in acts of disobedience for which we use the plural, "sins." This problem exists in our human life. We cannot perfectly understand its source, but in our own experience we know the paradox of its inevitability and our responsibility.

At the present time, as a result of the tragedies of the modern world, particularly in the terrible wars in which we have participated, there has come a new realization of the profundity of this conception of the human predicament. We have realized more deeply not only our individual but also our social involvement in fallenness. That is why the view of man in the Bible has come to satisfy the need for self-understanding of so many who have returned to the Christian faith.

The first Christians were no Utopia-builders. They knew that our position is desperate. They recognized human self-centeredness. They saw that this came as separation from God, which made life difficult and death a disaster. They sensed that we stand together, helpless in the presence of a holy God who has every right simply to judge us. He could leave us to our own ultimate destruction, *but He did not.*

Instead, He sends His Word to us in re-creation even as He sent His Word in creation. God makes possible our restoration to life with Him through giving His uttermost gift. He actually comes to share the whole experience which we enjoy and suffer. He enters the world to do something which was absolutely necessary to overcome the basic disaster of human life.

This then is the understanding of the Act of God in Jesus which the early Church and Christians always have believed happened. They have explained it in different ways. This does not mean so much contradiction and conflict as the enrichment of Christian thought. It is to be noticed that this Act of God has a focus in the death and Resurrection of Jesus. It has sometimes disturbed Christians that in the Creeds the confession of faith passes immediately from the Incarnation to the Cross. The reason for this is that the Cross is the result of the whole life of Jesus. What He did and what He said brought Him there, and His doing and His saying was the first obedience in utter perfection which God ever had from man.

This is the reason why we think of Jesus as the Second Adam and the New Creation. In more abstract terms, Jesus is referred to in theology as "Man" rather than "a man." His humanity is representative rather than merely individual. His life is God's beginning of the human race all over again. This is part of the significance of the Virgin Birth. Since men always find themselves judged by perfection, they quite naturally destroyed Jesus.

The death of Jesus and its consequences are proclaimed as the very special act whereby God freed man. This is the astonishing belief of Christians. They declare that at the very moment of man's utter rejection of God's purposes, He made a way out for them. Sometimes this is explained as the necessary sacrifice of a perfect human life to satisfy the justice of God. We owe God a death because of our misuse of life, and Jesus paid the debt. Frequently this belief is portrayed crudely, and sometimes in such a way that the love of God is obscured by His wrath. This will not be so if we remember as in the New Testament that it was God Himself who paid the price; it was not the vengeful Deity asking for propitiation by an innocent man.

To understand the saving Act of God in Jesus, it is urgent that we perceive the unity between the Cross and the Resurrection. In the New Testament, the truth is firmly grasped that these events are essentially one. The faithful death of Christ makes the Resurrection inevitable. God answers Jesus' obedience by reversing His destruction. Equally it is the Resurrection which gives meaning to the death of Christ. All the powers of evil—sin, pain, and death—converge upon Jesus and are destroyed in Him, destroyed for us. The Resurrection is portrayed not as a solitary event happening only to Jesus. It happened to Jesus for us. In the New Testament the Resurrection is a gift. The Risen Life of Jesus is bestowed upon men. We can enter into it as into a new state of existence.

When we understand the life of Jesus in this fashion, as the earliest Christians did, then we see what they meant when they said He was the Word of God. This is God's Act of reclamation. This is God speaking through a deed making sense out of human life again. It is important to perceive that the saving power in the life of Christ should be thought of as the re-creation of all things in which we can participate, and not simply as redemption from sin. Redemption is the beginning; eternity the end. This reveals God's nature. God is the sort of God who would do this for fallen man. Thus God speaks through this re-creative Act in Christ as He spoke to make the worlds.

In the last analysis all of this depends on the reality of the Resurrection. Have we a right to believe that Jesus was raised from the dead? If so, in what sense is this true? This is no place to go into the evidences of the Resurrection extensively. This has been done time and again and done exceptionally well in a study called *The Resurrection of Christ*,[2] by the present Archbishop of York.

[2] A. M. Ramsey, *The Resurrection of Christ* (Philadelphia: Westminster Press, 1946).

We will never believe in the Resurrection or in any other divine act because it is absolutely demonstrable. However, it is too often implied that faith is "a leap in the dark," that it is a daring and gloriously absurd act of trust in God which is contrary to all the appearances. This is not the understanding of faith in the best Christian tradition. Faith is a reasonable thing if the object of our faith can be called "The Word of God," particularly in the Greek sense. Consistently with this, when we approach the question of the Resurrection we must take into account all of the evidence. We must consult the Biblical records with all of their confusion, which would naturally come from such a shocking experience. We must also recognize the transformation of personality in the Apostles whereby they were changed from frightened, hidden men to bold preachers of the Gospel.

Faith is also greatly assisted by authority. This is an uncongenial word to a modern, democratically oriented Christian. This reaction, however, is the result of misunderstanding. Authority in the Christian Church is not coercion. It is the witness of a community in history. The Church has a right to speak about the Resurrection. That is to say, we find in the sacrifice of martyrs, the holiness of humble men, the conversion of notable sinners, and all the other typical Christian manifestations the recurrence of the life of

Christ—"The Lord is glorious in his saints." We also can be reassured by the persistence of the Church in spite of the powerful and ingenious devices which have been employed to destroy it. This bears witness to the presence of divine power in its life. Then there are the results of the Christian faith such as the great developments in medicine and learning and the way in which millions have taken not only history but their own lives more seriously. When we make up our minds about Jesus, when we decide whether or not He is risen from the dead, such facts as these are there to guide us.

In the last analysis, however, faith is a personal act. It is an act of trust. When we receive the Word of God, we do so because we dare to have confidence in Jesus Christ. This is an act of the whole man. It is moral—it is an act of decision. It is rational—it is an act of thought. It is emotional—it is an act of love. Faith in Jesus Christ belongs to the same kind of discovery of truth that we experience in our deepest relationships. We cannot know another person unless he reveals himself to us and we trust him enough to perceive his nature.

It has been the witness of Christians that when they have dared to believe in Jesus as the Risen Redeemer, they actually found Him present to them. This does not mean that they all had vivid mystical experiences, but rather that they made this discovery in more ordinary ways. Some of them apparently have had a special awareness of His presence, but for most it has been a meeting of a different sort. It has normally had an Incarnational pattern. The Word was made flesh, and it is the habit of the Word to enflesh Himself. He meets men in various promised ways, in their sacramental gatherings, in the declaration of God's saving acts, in the lives of Christians.

There have been many, however, who have not recognized the Word of God. One of the most terrible passages in the New Testament is that judgment in the prologue of the Fourth Gospel, "He came unto his own and his own received him not." It is hard for us who believe to conceive how this could be, yet surely it happened. As we read the story of the rejection of Jesus, we find one persistent element. The One for whom they were looking was someone entirely different from Jesus. They had a picture of the Deliverer which was not the figure of the One who came.

This has many implications for us all. At the highest level, it means that we should continually correct our picture of Jesus with constant reference to all we know about Him in His life and in His effect in history. In a much more minor matter, it means that the actual visual picture of Jesus which we carry in our imagination is very important. It has come to pass in the last century, and indeed ever since the religious paintings of the Renaissance, that Jesus has been portrayed in a very naturalistic way. We think of Him as a bearded figure robed rather like a Greek. We must remember as we have noted before that God apparently did not intend for us to know accurately the details of Jesus' appearance. Perhaps what we need to restore—and modern art can do it—is the image of Jesus such as can be found in the icons of the East, the Romanesque sculpture of France, the stained glass of the early Gothic. In these media Christians have tried to portray Jesus in His eternal aspect, the wonder and strangeness of His life as the God-Man.

In whatever way we imagine Jesus, it must be adequate to bear the message that this One has uttered the creative redeeming Word of God in His life. Above all, this must be an image which is capable of expressing *eschatological* truth. This word is one which the modern Christian should know. If he can understand the jargon of psychology which so often produces in him a sense of meaninglessness, he might well learn the terms of theology which can save his sense of meaning. Eschatology is simply the doctrine of the last things. The New Testament is saturated with a sense of the impending end of all things. This is something which has become again very real to Christians.

The Christian finds that in Jesus the Word is spoken within history which will be spoken at the end of history. Jesus the Risen Lord simply must be the final Word. With this in mind, the Christian dares to face problems and tragedies of human existence, for he has found the real meaning of personality and history in his Lord.

Receiving Jesus the Word of God is not a once-for-all experience. It is an ever-recurring event in the lives of Christians. It is important that we should be present at the times and places when it happens. These are very predictable, for we have it on His own authority when they occur. We shall now proceed to consider them. We shall seek to discover how we may receive the Word in the Bible, in the liturgy, and in preaching, and how the Word may be received from us in Christian life.

CHAPTER II

RECEIVING THE WORD OF GOD IN THE BIBLE

THE BIBLE is called Holy. The very title indicates that there is something different about the book. Here is a volume of many volumes which for centuries has been revered. The reason for this title must be that something unusual has happened, or is supposed to happen, when the book is read. What is the nature of the distinctiveness of the Bible that would admit its being called Holy?

To answer this question it is necessary to know what the book actually is. During the past century there has been a major development in the knowledge of the Bible so that we are in a better position to interpret it than in any century since the canon was determined. Biblical scholarship during this period has been a tremendous work involving men of all nations. Simply as an intellectual feat it commands respect.

Modern Christians have the duty to learn as much of what has been discovered in this field as they are capable of understanding so that they may better use the Scriptures. Naturally not all of us can be scholars, but in an era when there is reasonably good general education, the basic principles of Biblical learning are within the grasp of most people.

The recent study of the Bible has had many aspects. One of the most fascinating has been archeology. It has involved most careful and meticulous scientific work. It has resulted in the excavation of ancient sites, and the search for early manuscripts. Recently this work has captured the imagination of the whole world by the discovery of the Dead Sea Scrolls and the remnants of the community from which they came.

An even more demanding discipline than archeology is Biblical criticism. First, there is textual criticism which, as the term implies, is the effort to reconstruct the original documents. This is often done by a comparison of manuscripts, and requires the most careful linguistic learning. We now have texts of the Bible in the original tongues which are vastly more accurate than the sources available to the translators of the King James Version in the seventeenth century. However, scholars cannot be expected to reach any final agreement on the text because the existing sources are too remote from the originals. The notes on variant readings in any modern Greek New Testament manifest the problem. In spite of the fact that the work of textual critics will never be finally done there is a really impressive consensus in their conclusions. No one need worry about being seriously misled as to the reading of any important passage.

The work of the textual critic is further advanced by the literary critic. His task is to examine the language and composition of the books, to make judgments about the date, authorship, sources, and other such problems. Another special kind of study has lately been developed called form criticism. This is a very adventurous kind of scholarship which seeks with apparent success to discover the oral and written traditions behind the Gospels. It has helped to show the relationship of the Bible to the Church. It has revealed how the memories of Jesus were cherished in the earliest churches and used in primitive preaching and worship.

Biblical critics of all these sorts have pursued their investigations passionately. The dialogue that has taken place among them has been very creative. It has resulted not only in careful linguistic and expository studies, but also in the production of numerous fine new translations such as those of Weymouth, Moffatt, Goodspeed, Knox, and the great corporate effort in the Revised Standard Version.

There is another task in Biblical studies which is never done. This is Biblical theology. It is necessary to know not only what the Bible says, but also what the Bible means. This is the particular concern of many Christian thinkers at the present time. It is now being said that we have come into the "post-critical" period; that is to say, we must now take the work of the scholars of previous decades and make sense out of it for Christian faith.

The ordinary layman, and even the theological student and clergyman, may well be appalled when he realizes the vastness of the work of Biblical studies. He may even despair of ever being able to understand it at all. Most of us cannot be competent in this field. We must humbly rely on the judgment of specialists. However, the churchman who can read news magazines can find his way easily through the popular interpretations of the Scriptures which are now offered. One of the first tasks in the work of receiving the Word of God in the Bible is simply reading and study.

Beyond any scholarly considerations, any understanding of the Bible must take into account two essential facts about it: it is the book of Jesus Christ, and it is the book of the Church.

The Bible is the book of Jesus Christ. It exists because of the impact of His life. The motivation for creating it comes from Jesus through His disciples. This book was not written as "holy scripture" in its origin. To deal quickly with certain obvious and illuminating facts, we should remember that the New Testament chronologically begins with the Epistles of St. Paul, which were written in about the middle of the first century as exhortation, interpretation, and admonition to young churches. The Gospels are the compilation from many sources of the oral traditions about Jesus which the Church wrote down so that they would not be lost. All of the other books of the New Testament were written for special purposes. It is apparent that Christians felt impelled to preserve the memories and interpretations of the earliest disciples. But can it be said that the Old Testament is the book of Jesus Christ? This indeed is true. The Old Testament, when it is bound together with the New, becomes a different book. It is no longer the Hebrew Scriptures. It is the preface to Jesus Christ. It should not be forgotten that the Old Testament was the Scripture of Jesus. Its insights and imperatives determined His life, and He is its fulfillment. Therefore, it is necessary for Christians to saturate themselves with its message in order to understand their Lord.

The Bible is also the book of the Church. One very

obvious fact is frequently ignored by people who revere the Bible: that is, that it was the Church which determined its content. This work was not complete until the middle of the fourth century. A multitude of writings about Jesus and the Church had to be sifted before the canon was decided. The history of this process is a fascinating but complicated study. Obviously this does not mean that the Word of God did not exist until the fourth century. It means that the Word of God is a living thing and that its existence for all of those years when the content of the Bible was not finally determined was in the continuing witness of Christians. This was the origin of the literature. Since it was the corporate decision of the Christian community that certain books belonged in Holy Scripture, the authority of the books depends upon the authority of the Church. It is equally true that the authority of the Church depends upon the authority of the Bible, for it is the message of this book that keeps creating the Church. The Church is what it is because the Bible is what it is—both are inseparable.

The Bible is the book of Jesus and the book of His Church. Receiving the Word of God in the Bible depends upon our apprehension of these two facts. When a Christian accepts them he reads the book with a special purpose and a special result. It can never be to him simply "living literature." It is indeed a book of fascinating stories and, in our great English translation, a book of moving beauty. There are some parts of it which are fascinating old tales. These can be appreciated legitimately as such. But this is not enough. There is an earnestness about the relationship of the Christian and his Bible. He simply must know all he can about Jesus Christ because he is in constant relation to Him through his faith and worship. He has the greatest passion for the exact text and interpretation because he should know as nearly as he can everything about the Word of God in the words. He does not, however, read alone. He reads as a member of the Body of Christ.

There have been quarrels throughout history about the propriety of "individual interpretation." One of the principles of the Reformation in contrast to the mind of the medieval Church was that the Bible should be available to every man. This is clearly valid if we mean that no one should be denied access to the book. If, however, it is meant that any man simply by taking up the Bible can immediately understand what it means, this is surely untrue. Even on the simple ground of Biblical studies, we must learn before we interpret. Furthermore, we need to know the history of the Bible in the Church. Over the centuries this book has had definite effects in the life of the

Christian community. The Church has developed a sense of proportion about it. For instance, all of the books of the Bible could not possibly be of equal worth. The violent book of Esther cannot possibly be as valuable as the compassionate book of Hosea. Certain passages in the Psalms which contain vicious cursing of enemies cannot possibly be read in the same way as the Sermon on the Mount. In the last analysis, it is in the Church's experience of the living Lord and her knowledge of His presence that the Bible must be read. One of the first principles of receiving the Word is to read the words of the Bible through Jesus Christ our Lord.

It would be an interesting project to undertake to explain how each book of the Bible may be rightly read, or even how each type of book should be approached. This task is far too vast for this book. There is, however, an even more basic question which must be considered: in what sense can we find the revelation of God in the Bible?

First, we must consider the nature of revelation. In order to do so we must begin with a sense of the nature of God. Any being who can be called *God* must be worshipful. Any being who is worshipful must transcend the worshipper. We cannot bow before our equals. If God is holy, how can we know Him? Surely this cannot be done by our investigation. The initiative must be on the other side. We can understand Him only when He shows Himself. We have considered this matter when we saw earlier in what way Jesus communicates the nature of God. An apprehension of the fact that He is the center of revelation is necessary to the understanding of revelation in the Bible. When God reveals Himself, He does so in terms of human life. It is a living action in history. This should destroy two false conceptions of revelation sometimes held which corrupt the understanding of the Bible.

The first misunderstanding is that revelation is by dictation, that the Word of God is to be found in utterances about Him which are contained in this book. Revelation comes through events. The Bible is essentially a history book. It contains evidences of what occurred through many centuries. This is plainly the professed purpose of the historical books such as Exodus, Joshua, Judges, the Kings. However accurate or inaccurate as history, they attempt to recount significant events and to interpret them theologically. The other books of the Bible should also be understood historically. The Psalms are the prayer book of the Hebrew people and show how their attitude to God developed through the years of encounter with Him in their glorious and tragic history. The prophets were not oracles uttering abstract truth. They were men whose message was directed toward urgent ethical problems which confronted them in their own time. Part of the Book of Genesis reveals the state of mind of the priestly class as it sought to interpret the scientific opinion of about the year 900 B.C. In the New Testament we naturally have the memories about Jesus and the story of the primitive Church. The Epistles are, like the prophecies, directed to specific situations. The Revelation of St. John the Divine is a book written for the Church during the persecution under Nero. When we read the words of the books of the Bible, we are not finding the sayings which the Holy Ghost whispered into the ears of the writers. We are witnessing the living response, made indeed through the power of the Spirit, by the people of God to God Himself as He dealt with them in history.

The second misunderstanding is to regard the Bible primarily as the record of a developing idea of God. We do find that the concept of God changes from that of a vengeful tribal deity to the God and Father of Jesus Christ. However, the perspective is wrong if we think of this change as something which the Hebrews did as they made their quest for the truth about Yahweh. The Bible perspective is the opposite. This is something which God did in His quest for the Hebrews; indeed, in His quest for the whole of the human race. The Hebrews knew that they were a peculiar people not because of their special religious genius, but because of the way in which God was treating them. They were an insignificant nation, and many of the events in their history were in size of small consequence, yet they were fraught with momentous import. For instance, when Israel came out of Egypt, this was apparently an exodus of a small group of persecuted Semites escaping from the Pharoah and eventually entering the Holy Land. The importance of this event (contrary to the fantastic portrayals of Hollywood) lies not in a series of marvels and spectacular movements of masses of people, but in the salvation of a people of God through an act of God, whereby He showed that He was their Deliverer. This sort of thing happened again and again in Hebrew history. We read the Bible most truly when we understand it as the record of the reaction of men to God's mighty acts, which may not be humanly very impressive.

The true understanding of the Bible leads us to recognize that there is a holy history within history. The Christian does not learn its events objectively, but as a participant in it. He receives it as his family history. This is true both of the Old Testament and the New Testament. In this connection it is important to point out that the Church of God is the whole people of

God. It is time to discard that unfortunate teaching about Pentecost as "the birthday of the Church." It is also a mistake to say that Jesus founded the Church. God founded the Church. God called His people in the dim mists of antiquity. Surely they numbered the great shapes of Abraham, Isaac, and Jacob. Certainly the Psalms were its prayers and the prophets its teachers. This is what Jesus believed. He was not founding, but re-founding, the Church. He made this plain by choosing the twelve as counterparts to the rulers of the twelve tribes of Israel. On Pentecost the people of God was empowered by the Spirit of God. In this history of the people of God we participate. It is continuous from the Old Testament through the New, even to us. In consequence the people of God in the Old Testament are our people. Christians are spiritually Hebrews in origin. As we acknowledge this history as our own we find God's revelation. We see how He dealt with the folk of the Old Covenant and of the New, and learning this we can understand how He deals with us now. Revelation is thus not abstract, propositional. In the Bible there is a dynamic experience, a real personal encounter between God and His people—of which I am one, you are one.

There is now a strong theological movement on the continent of Europe called "demythologization."

This is originally a Germanic development, and its chief exponent is Rudolph Bultmann. It has gained considerable currency in American religious circles. It is the contention of this school that the Christian faith must be reinterpreted in modern terms. The world view of the Bible is no longer tenable. In the Old and New Testaments the universe is portrayed in three levels: above is the region of goodness—Heaven; below is the region of evil—Hell; in between is the region of man—Earth. Divine beings and demonic beings ascend and descend between these spheres influencing the life of man. The advent of such powers is the occasion of miracle. The demythologizers claim that this pattern can no longer be taken seriously. We live in a world which is understood by all intelligent men scientifically. The world view of the Bible can never be accepted in our society. Therefore, all of the elements of "myth" must be removed from the presentation of the Gospel, and the proclamation translated into the current language of existentialism.

This is a very bold program, and it has engaged the efforts of some of our most brilliant theologians. They have sought to salvage from the Biblical writings what they consider to be the essential value, namely that God does encounter man in Jesus Christ with a radical demand. But such mattters as the Virgin Birth, the Resurrection, and the Last Judgment are discarded.

Demythologization has been criticized on many

grounds. The controversy is one of the most vigorous in contemporary theology. The critics of this theory object that in religion myth is not necessarily evil, and surely not avoidable. Furthermore, they claim that it is assuming too much to conclude that the scientific world view at present is the final world view. Obviously the science of 1960 is not the science of 1930. Another generation may have a totally different conception of the nature of the world. The critics also are not convinced that existentialist categories, however valuable, will have any greater permanence than the thought forms of other philosophies. In short, demythologization fails because it does the very thing in our century which it seeks to eliminate from the Bible; namely, it entangles the Word of God with the thought forms of a particular age.

There is one other questionable assumption in demythologization. It is not at all certain that modern man cannot take seriously a three-level world. We do not live in it scientifically, but we do psychologically. Above is the region of light. When we are joyful, we look up. Below is the region of darkness and dirt. When we are depressed, we are downcast. This is the language of poetry and of everyday speech. It is not necessary for us to accept the world view of the Bible literally; in fact it is quite probable that many of the writers of Scripture did not do so themselves.

It is, however, inevitable that we should use the normal language of human experience when we seek to express the deepest human experience, namely our encounter with God. Is it so incredible that God when He communicated His Word to men in human flesh also accommodated Himself to human psychology? Even the Ascension, a favorite target of the demythologizers, does not seem preposterous, even if we do not know how, or in what sense, Jesus "went up." There may well have been some sign given the Apostles in terms of our three-level world view, which helped them to know the destiny of Jesus as Lord.

The cult of demythologization forces us to consider two categories which are in constant use in the Bible: miracle and myth. The intelligent Christian should face the question of what he thinks about them.

The Bible is full of miracle stories. In fact, the whole central affirmation of the Gospel focuses on a miracle—the Resurrection of Jesus. First of all, it should be recognized that all of these stories are not of the same sort. The miracles of Elisha are different from the miracles of Jesus. Making an ax-head float on a stream is different from healing a man with a withered hand. Even in the Gospels it appears probable that some miracles such as the blasting of the fig tree are unlikely occurrences. Others such as certain healings, particularly of mental disease, might be understood clinically at the present time. It is interesting that in the Creeds, only three miracles, the Virgin Birth, the Resurrection, and the Ascension, are singled out for the confession of faith.

It is not our purpose here to argue this question at length, but simply to point out that it is characteristic of the Christian religion to be Incarnational. When the Word of God is made flesh, it is for the purpose of re-creating all things which are made by Him. If we reject the category of miracle we maneuver ourselves into a position of believing that we know what God can and cannot do. We further assume that a static situation exists in creation even when God undertakes a special act of revelation and rescue. We do not need to believe in all miracle tales, but it would seem that it is necessary for a Christian to accept the fact that his Lord was not ultimately destroyed, even in body, by the powers of evil. The great miracle is Jesus Christ Himself. He is more of a wonder and more of an improbability in His very being than any story told about anything that He did.

The category of myth is also characteristically Biblical. A myth is essentially a pattern story which seeks to show the meaning of existence through a narrative. It is employed by simple people and also by philosophers. When we read the great myths of the book of Genesis, for instance, we can immediately sense its value. The stories of Adam and Eve, Cain and Abel, Noah and the Flood, the Tower of Babel— all of these are profound interpretations of recurring situations. They are so typical that in a certain sense they are truer than history. The most profound experiences of human life are very difficult to express abstractly. Myth solves the problem. There is a further question, however; that is, accepting stories which were intended to be actual history as though they were myths. For instance, it has been shown that the history in the books of Kings is far from accurate. Does this mean that they should be thrown out of the canon? This is not necessary because these books, which were doubtless not written by liars, but by inadequate historians, preserve an essential principle of the theology of history. They show how the ultimate meaning of human life and of political life is to be judged in terms of obedience to God's laws. For us the books of Kings are books of myths, but our own history could be written and read by the same principles.

What of the actual language of the Bible? Should we seek to discard it or to reinterpret it in other completely different terms? Or is there something essential even in the words, or at least some of them, to the communication of the Word?

Many years ago it was thought that the language in which the Bible was written was literally the language of the Holy Spirit. This was obviously a crude mistake, but there is a certain sense in which it is true. The meaning of language has recently become both a scholarly and a popular concern. Everyone is talking about semantics. It has been recognized that words and their use are not simple signs. A language is formed by a culture. It can express the point of view of that culture. It is an historical and social thing. There are some experiences that are better expressed in one language than another. In fact, there are certain things that cannot be said in some languages. This has been a problem for translators of the Bible. Some concepts in the New Testament have no words for them in Oriental languages. The English translator may be reduced to the expedient of intruding, for instance, an English word into the Japanese New Testament because it has no Japanese equivalent. This has been the case ever since the human race began speaking. It has profound connotations in the question of receiving the Word of God.

The language of the Bible, particularly of the New Testament, is a different language from any other. It was formed by many factors. Behind it is the whole of the Old Testament with its sense of the importance of history, the intervention of God, the reality of the moral law, and the final destiny of creation being an act of God. Such concepts are certainly not characteristic of Greek literature. Yet the language of the New Testament is Greek, and many of the ideas in the New Testament are Greek. This is particularly true of the very idea of the Word of God. The New Testament, therefore, represents a new intersection of two cultures, of two languages.

St. Paul speaks of Jesus as coming in "the fulness of times." This means that Jesus came at the right time. Surely one aspect of the right time is that He came at that point in history when the language was available to express the meaning of His coming. The right time implies the right language. This is one reason why good theology must always be Biblical theology. Rather than forsaking the world view of the first century because it is not our contemporary world view, is it not necessary for the Christian to have two world views, two cultures, two languages? Whenever there is a group of concerned people with a special message to communicate they will have their own language. This language must be learned. It is best learned by continual association with the literature which makes it.

In the Church the language of the Word of God

is to be found in the Bible and in the liturgy. In our
encounter with these sources, we carry on with them
what may be considered a great conversation. This
language may sometime have a tremendous world importance. Communication in this era has become
difficult between peoples. The great gulf between
East and West has made it difficult for us to understand each other. Sometimes reading the accounts of
statements by Russian folk we feel that we cannot
believe what we see. The categories are strange and
objectionable to us. But the Russian Christian can
understand the American Christian, at least in the
realm of the language of the Church. This may be
one of the binding unities which may eventually save
mankind.

Now all of this has profound implications for Christian education. One of the tasks which has to be un-
dertaken by every responsible Christian man, woman,
and child is becoming thoroughly familiar with all
that makes the language of the Word of God. We
need to know the stories which provide the thought
patterns of the Bible. We need to feel the force of the
events which are interpreted in the language. We need
to become thoroughly familiar with the persons who
spoke what is there recorded, until we come to think

of these as acquaintances or better, members of the family of God together with us. Thus in our membership in the great Church we become provided with the vehicle whereby we can receive the revelation of God in the Word of God in its deepest meaning.

This task is never done. It means special kinds of work for some. Surely for many it is going to involve the learning of the original tongues, Hebrew and Greek. Within the memory of this generation, there were laymen who daily read their Greek New Testaments. This would naturally be the very best kind of Bible reading, but it is impossible for most people. At the present time, there are many versions of the Scriptures which can be of great assistance to any English-speaking person. The King James Version is part of the literary and religious heritage of us all. It is by all odds still the best translation to be used in the services of the Church because of the perfection of its prose. What inadequacies there are in interpretation are more than made up for by its beauty. That very beauty, however, may create another problem. We may enjoy the book so much that it does not make its impact. We may need to have the refreshing experience of reading familiar passages in the contemporary speech. The new translations when they are done by one scholar are inclined to be more vivid and arresting than those done by commissions. They

are, however, naturally permeated by the characteristics of an individual personality. It is good to have
more than one of them so that the proclivities of the
translator may be detected.

When we become thoroughly familiar with the
Bible, when we have permitted it to govern our ways
of thinking, through forming the patterns of our
mind, then we can understand more deeply the reality
of God's revelation of Himself within it. This is a
strange and different book. It can never be proved by
any logical process that the history there recorded is
a history of divine acts. One either sees it or he does
not. One of the peculiar problems for the Christian
to understand is how many Biblical scholars are not believing and practicing Christians. That is obviously
not because they did not know the Bible. The reason
was that they did not relate themselves to it by faith.
One must approach this book with openness of heart,
expectation, and trust if anything is to happen to him.

It is clearly the witness of the Church that within
the Bible is to be found a special revelation. God can
be found in nature and in history, if He has been found
first in the Bible. There is much in the world of evil
and of confusion. The Bible helps us to sort out which
phenomena reveal God and which do not. The Biblical Christian then does not become narrow-minded
because he believes that the Word of God is in the

Bible. He freely acknowledges that the same Word which is presented to him there is the Word which lightens every man who comes into the world. Rather than being exclusive, he is given an impulse to go beyond the Bible and expectantly to search for truth wherever it is to be found.

If the Bible does indeed contain the Word of God, if it is the revelation of God, then clearly it is the Christian's duty to bear witness to the right use of it. There are certain typical mistakes which must be rejected.

The Bible must never be permitted to be regarded with superstitious awe. Many people regard the book itself with a certain peculiar reverence. Encouragement is given to this attitude by the exotic way in which it is published. It looks unlike other books. The edges are gilded, the covers made of fine limp leather from Morocco, the pages of "India" paper (formerly made in China, now in America). It is a proper object for display, an important symbol. It is not strange that people hesitate to set objects on it, and honor it in handling it, if not in reading it. It may become a religious symbol of the same sort in which the flag is a patriotic symbol. Sometimes the book actually has been used in magical ways as in "biblio-

mancy." Some Christians who sought to find the will
of God have simply opened the Bible, closed their
eyes, put down their fingers on a passage, and attributed what they read to the Holy Spirit as His
guidance. It must have been something like this even
St. Augustine did when he heard the voice of a chant-
ing child saying "Take and read," and opened the
Bible to read St. Paul's exhortation to a pure life,
which converted him. In that case the effect was
fortunate, but there have been many amusing and
even disastrous results from this abuse.

Much more damaging than this obviously ignorant
misunderstanding is fundamentalism. It does not seem
possible that this error could be revived. Unfortunately it has been.

Many years ago there were people who believed in
the verbal infallibility of the Bible. They actually
claimed that the Word of God was identical with the
words of the book. They could not tolerate the idea
that there are mistakes in the Scriptures. They refused
to recognize even the obvious contradictions in certain
stories in the Bible. They had a conception of inspira-
tion by the dictation of the Holy Spirit. The Christian
religion was for them a religion of the book. It cannot be denied that among people of this point of view
there was much saintly life. They were often deeply
devoted to Jesus Christ. When Biblical criticism was

developed, and when the geological and biological sciences produced their new discoveries about the origin of the world and human life, they recoiled in horror from such ideas. They believed that their faith was threatened because the infallibility of the Bible was threatened. A great battle ensued with tragic results in certain parts of the Christian community.

About the turn of the century, when these issues were very vivid, those who still believed in Biblical infallibility came to be called fundamentalists. As time passed it became more and more evident that their position was completely untenable. This was not necessarily a victory for "liberalism." Many times in his zeal not to be obscurantist the liberal lost all sense of Biblical authority. Religion then degenerated into mere moralism. The liberal's inadequate response has now largely been replaced by a recovery of enlightened Biblical theology. This recovery came in part from the remarkable revival on the continent of Europe called the Theology of Crisis. These matters are not the concern of the academic alone. Every Christian can profit by the development of stronger affirmation which has characterized recent Christian thought.

Now, to our distress, we discover that there is a revival of fundamentalism. It must be left to historians of the future to discover all of the causes of this strange phenomenon. Certainly one reason is the desire for security which obsesses so many people today. We live in anxiety over the future. We have a feeling of futility in the present. To be able to lay hold on a book and to claim for it divine infallibility gives the modern fundamentalist reassurance. He is greatly assisted at the present time by the growth of a revivalism strongly supported by modern methods of mass communication. He is also encouraged by the appearance of new publications with all of the style and symbolic format of scholarly periodicals. With all of this appearing in our midst, we may well be anxious lest the fruits of a century of devoted labor in Biblical studies should be lost. This is a particularly unfortunate development at the time when so many intellectuals are inquiring about the Christian faith. A toleration of obscurantism as a legitimate Christian position may prevent them from seeing a better way.

The Bible will survive all misunderstandings of it. It will survive because of what truly happens to those who read it. The Word of God comes to man through it. It produces the transformation of their lives as day by day they receive its power.

CHAPTER III

RECEIVING THE WORD OF GOD IN THE LITURGY

CAN THE WORD of God be received in the liturgy? Apparently not, or at least not properly, if the protest of many earnest men is to be believed. Rites and ceremonies, they say, stifle the Spirit and keep men from hearing the voice of God. The priest is the natural enemy of the prophet. If in churches which employ liturgy the Word of God is heard at all, it is in spite of, and not because of, the forms. Such convictions are likely to be held with strong assurance, and can be found reappearing again and again in history with great destructive force. Furthermore, they have deep Biblical roots.

The prophets of the Old Testament often inveighed against the priests. They condemned the solemn services and the careful ceremonial practices which covered the unrighteousness of hypocrites. Jesus Himself denounced the same manifestations, pointing out

71

time and again how men can make the Word of God
of no effect through their traditions. Among His chief
enemies were the priests. He was finally bought by
them from Judas with thirty pieces of silver.

With the weight of such a record, reformers in
many and varying Christian traditions have repudiated
some or all of liturgy in the Church. The iconoclasts
in the East found representations of divine events
idolatrous. Calvinists destroyed altars and images,
whitewashed the walls of medieval churches, and
smashed the stained glass. The austere silent worship
of the Quaker emerged. All of this and countless more
can be found to declare that there can be deep and
lasting enmity between the believers in the Word of
God and the traditional worship of the Christian
Church.

In the presence of this formidable array, churchmen of liturgical traditions may be tempted to become
defensive. Such a reaction is both unnecessary and un-
faithful. It is a denial of Jesus' own practice. He participated in the rich worship of His own people,
upholding it even to the point of the violent cleansing
of the temple. He said not one word against the rites
and ceremonies of Hebrew religion except in their
abuse. Above all it should never be forgotten that He
took the occasion of a ceremonial meal, in some way
connected with the Passover, as the moment for the

oblation of Himself. He used the liturgical eating and drinking of a traditional feast as the means of offering His death for redemption. What He did by example and institution has become the common norm for Christians. Most of Christ's disciples have found liturgical practice inevitable and natural.

A definition of the liturgy is necessary for our discussion because the term has been used in different ways. There is precedent for using the word solely in connection with the Eucharist. In the Eastern Church this service is simply called the Divine Liturgy. But there is better reason to give the term a wider meaning to include all of the words and actions of corporate worship. This is the principle of the Book of Common Prayer, and we shall accept it. The reason for so doing is that the whole worship of the Church is best considered as one united action. The Eucharist is indeed the central and supreme focus, but the rest of the sacramental functions and offices of prayer are related to the one divine center of it all, Jesus Christ.

This is an age of the rediscovery of the liturgy. Throughout the whole of Christendom there has been a new apprehension of the meaning and importance of worship. This has crossed the boundaries of denominationalism. It has even created a new kind of

Christian unity as men on the opposite sides of the great chasm between Romanism and Protestantism have become indebted to each other for new insights. Almost everyone now has heard of the Liturgical Movement. However, there are serious misconceptions about its nature. It is emphatically not just the "enrichment" of worship by the addition of more paraphernalia. Neither is it an archeological regression, merely an attempt to restore lost uses from other ages of the Church.

The Liturgical Movement began in the nineteenth century in France as a research into medieval music. The great Dom Guéranget of the monastery of Solesmes fostered these studies so effectively that interest spread throughout the whole of Europe. The movement passed into Belgium and Germany, where great centers of the rediscovery of the whole liturgy developed. It was no longer simply a musical research. It became investigation of the Biblical grounds of Christian worship and the practice of the early days of the Church. This produced a complete re-evaluation of the understanding of the liturgy for many Roman Catholics. Furthermore, a concern arose for the communication of these insights on a popular and pastoral level. At the present time, the work which has been accomplished by Roman Catholic exponents of this school has become the possession of men of all communions.

One of the strange characteristics of the Liturgical Movement is the way in which it has sprung up in many different places during the same period, sometimes developing simultaneously very similar ideas in separate Christian traditions. In the Anglican communion, there has been a tremendous wave of interest in the recovery of better ways of worship. Curiously, many of the goals of the Roman leaders of the Liturgical Movement were the goals of the Reformers who produced the Book of Common Prayer. Anglicans have come to value their forms of corporate worship more as they realize that other Christians are seeking the same thing.

There is hardly a Church which has been untouched by this development. On the continent of Europe there have been notable revivals of worship in the Calvinist Churches of France and Holland, centering especially in the Taizé community of French Protestant men living under a rule of life in a village near the ancient monastery of Cluny. In the Church of Scotland for many years there has been a revived concern in these matters. This now focuses on the Iona community, a group of Presbyterians who combine work in industrial areas with study and devotion part of the year on the venerable island of St. Columba in the Inner Hebrides. The instances could be multiplied many times over. When any movement develops in this way, Christians should recognize that it is in some degree the work of the Holy Spirit. Therefore, they have an obligation to make as full a response to it as they can.

What are the principles of the Liturgical Movement? There are several great motifs which run through all its manifestations. First, the Liturgical Movement declares the worship of the Church to be action. Second, it emphasizes the necessity of corporateness. Third, it seeks to make the liturgy intelligible. Fourth, it revives the interpretation of its meaning as it was clearly understood in the first days of the Church. These principles pertain directly to our concern. The application of each of them directly enhances the awareness of the liturgy as a vehicle of the Word.

1. *Action*

One common mistake in regarding the liturgy is to consider it to be basically a form of words. This is the error of the medieval Church which thought of the Mass as something to be "said." It also misled the Reformers, who frequently composed verbose orders of worship. It has come down to us, and at the present time it is safe to say that the ordinary American churchgoer, especially if he is a Protestant, thinks that he comes to church primarily to hear something. In actual fact, it must be remembered that the source of

Christian worship is Christ and what Christ did. Christ is the chief Actor in the drama. We participate in it as members of His Body, not a dead and passive thing, but a living reality. This implies that we should have a much more dynamic conception of the liturgy, that we should approach it with the feeling that something happens in the service of the Church. This is especially clear in the case of the Holy Communion, where we are doing things with bread and wine, obedient to Christ's action and example, in order that He may come to us and we to Him. In worship, whether it be in sacramental deeds, in reading of the Scripture, or in the experience of the sermon, we are engaged in great doings. This awareness that the Liturgical Movement has brought us should open our minds and hearts to the reception of Christ as the living creative Word of God, more fully than before.

2. *Corporateness*

In emphasizing the corporate nature of the action of the liturgy, the movement has given back to the people their proper function as participants in the worship of the Church. We can no longer be happy with the conception of a service which is delivered by one man to the congregation. Each Christian has his own ministry, but he exercises it properly only in relation to the whole company of the faithful. This saves the Church from individualism which prevents us from realizing our membership in Christ. Participation in worship opens up the personality to God's acts. As men become involved in the actions and words of the services, they are more able to apprehend the meaning of the Word which saturates all true Christian liturgy.

3. *Intelligibility*

The Liturgical Movement has sought to make all Christians understand the meaning of worship. This is a great problem at the present time. It is sad to say that most people who come to church do not understand very much of what goes on there. This is aggravated where it is the custom to use an unknown tongue. Many Roman Catholics are now urging a vernacular liturgy, and since this is not yet possible for them, they have introduced a common language into their services in various ways. Those of us who use our own tongue should not be too smug about the predicament of the Latin Church. King James' English may be at times very obscure to a modern American. Very often the whole structure of the liturgy is unintelligible because our folk have not been adequately instructed and because we have involved our worship with meaningless ceremonies. Sometimes there has been a veritable and deliberate cult of unintelligibility. The excuse given for this is that mysterious actions and inaudible words produce a "numinous" atmosphere appropriate to a great holy action. The "numinous" which is appropriate to Christian worship does not come from such cultic devices. It comes rather from a clear understanding of the awfulness of the action in which we are engaged. When a man becomes aware that he is actually meeting God in a service, he will have a sufficient sense of the holy. By developing careful explanation, by insisting on plain and clear words, actions, and symbols, the Liturgical Movement has helped the Church perceive the meaning of its own action.

4. *Revival*

The reason why the leaders of the Liturgical Movement look to the early days of the Church for guidance is manifold. During the Middle Ages, though the liturgy became magnificent, the understanding of it became corrupt. Individualism and superstition were rife. The Reformers in reaction often destroyed too much. The only way in which it is possible to restore the right meaning of corporate worship is to return to the roots. We have to find out from the New Testament what was the origin of our actions. We need to learn from the more objective mind of the Church of the Fathers how the liturgy was performed with meaning and simplicity. Singularly enough, in going back to these sources, we find Christian thought which is very congenial to the modern mind. Again this is a matter pertaining to the Word. It is essentially the rediscovery of the liturgy by reviving the Biblical conception of its nature, and learning from the ages when this conception was most perfectly accepted.

While the Liturgical Movement has opened up new possibilities for receiving the Word, there are still dangers to be avoided if we are to profit from its insight. These are the old mistakes which have always been criticized by reformers.

The first is romanticism. Liturgical worship can be made an escape from reality. The services of the Church are and should be beautiful. They remind us of the past and give a sense of security which comes from the symbols of a venerable institution. If we seek to hide ourselves from the anxieties of our time by retreating into a Neo-Gothic religion then we shall fail to find God. We may escape the awareness of His judgment. We may fail to recognize His will for His present world. Eventually our worship becomes unreal.

Estheticism is a further danger. The things of our worship ought to be beautiful. They should be repre-

sentative of the very best in art and music. They are,
however, supposed to speak of something beyond
themselves. When we focus our attention on them
simply as satisfying and lovely objects and actions, we
turn them into idols and prevent their speaking to us
of the things of God.

The liturgical Churches are sometimes accused of
formalism. This, unfortunately, is often valid. It is
possible, though not inevitable, to use forms of prayer
in such a fashion that we escape the necessity of decision and fail to feel the urgency which is often
present in more spontaneous traditions. Here again we
are using a device to prevent our hearing what God
would say.

In spite of the fact that liturgy can be abused, it is
both inevitable and powerful. Communication by
signs is necessary to man. He is going to employ them
when he deals with his fellow men and with God, because he is made as a sign-using creature. The fact
that this power can be abused does not mean that it
should be rejected. Furthermore, it should be recognized that it *is* a power. The very violence of the
objection to liturgy is an inverted witness to its importance. When rightly used it can have an extraordinary and immediate effect on the life of Christians.
It what way can it become a vehicle of the Word of
God?

The liturgy provides two special means of communication, *ritual* and *ceremonial*. These two words are frequently confused. Properly, ritual refers to the rite or words of a service; ceremonial pertains to the action and articles used in its performance. Ritual and ceremonial have been considered enemies of the Word of God, but when rightly used they are truly powerful vehicles of the Word of God.

Ritual, the words of the liturgy, has a profound effect upon participants in worship. When the services of the Church are repeated in the same form again and again, the repetition is not "vain." It is inevitable that the language used should become part of the subconscious life of the Christian. This is revealed in the experience we all have of using phrases from our Prayer Book in our common conversation. The ritual has become a part of our natural expression, which means that it has come to govern our thought processes.

In this connection, it would be well to sense the power of repetition. What we hear over and over again, even if we do not each time fully sense the whole meaning, begins to influence our lives. This is one of the principles of advertising. The reiteration of a radio or television commercial, the appearance of the same slogans week by week in magazines impel us to buy. In the Church there is the regular weekly and daily form of Common Prayer which does this same thing. Within this form there are certain oft-repeated words, such as the Lord's Prayer, the Creeds. They reappear in more than one context and each time drive their meaning deeper into our minds. What man has not had the unnerving experience of realizing that he was thinking about something else when he was saying the Lord's Prayer or the Creed? It is right to be shocked at such a self-discovery, yet that does not mean that nothing has happened. It is often in such familiar repetitions that the words become part of us. In fact, the man who strains to focus on every phrase may actually fail to absorb the liturgy.

The words of the ritual contain the Word of God. We are not now speaking solely of the many passages of actual Scripture which are part of it; rather we are thinking of the way in which the language has been created by the thought forms in which the revelation has come to us. As they become a part of our lives, they help to make the patterns of our decisions and to condition our spiritual response. This is of special importance in those great human crises when we desperately need to have something available to guide and strengthen us. The Word of God habitually received in the rites of the Church naturally emerges at such moments to determine our reactions when considered thought and feeling fail.

Ceremonial is as powerful a medium as ritual. This

is evident in certain immediately understood actions such as the handclasp, the kiss, the embrace. These ceremonies can be expressions too deep for words. They grow naturally out of the embodied life of man.

What is true of ordinary human behavior is also true in the liturgy. Certain elemental signs are used: washing in Baptism clearly means cleansing; the eating of bread and drinking of wine obviously signify union and communion; the laying on of hands in Confirmation bespeaks the fatherly act of blessing. These are basic actions which come from ordinary experience. In the liturgy they are transfigured in their use. Some other signs come directly from history. This is obvious with the cross, the inevitable symbol of the death and Resurrection of Jesus. Still others are functional, as in the case of the altar, which stands in the church as the chief focus and holy place because it is the table of Christ. Such ceremonial signs can reach us with an immediacy greater than speech, and therefore have a tremendous power in conveying to us the Word of God.

There is another type of symbolism which is very popular but less useful. This is the esoteric sign which does not have an obvious meaning. It is a symbolic puzzle. Some of these have considerable antiquity, such as the fish, which, as is well known, is an acrostic. The word for fish in Greek is *ichthus* (ιχθύς). The spelling is taken to represent the first letters of the words in a Greek sentence which reads, "Jesus Christ, Son of God, Saviour." In times of persecution such devices were doubtless useful methods of identification. Later on they became fascinating pious games. Too often these symbols did not represent the really important contribution of the heroes of the Church. For instance, the sign of St. Benedict was often a blackbird, because he was supposed to have been miraculously rescued from death by such a creature snatching away a piece of poisoned bread. Obviously there are more important memories of St. Benedict than this dubious tale.

This sort of symbolism is dangerous because it tends to make unnecessary mystery rather than clear communication. Indeed, there have been times when important symbols have been corrupted by their being reinterpreted in this manner. A serious instance is the explanation of Eucharistic vestments. There have been a multitude of meanings read into their use. Sometimes they have been taken to represent various incidents of the Passion. Also they have been interpreted as signs of Christian character: the alb standing for purity, the amice for the helmet of salvation, and even the chasuble, for charity which covers a multitude of sins. Quite obviously there is a real and valid historical reason for wearing Eucharistic vestments. They are historical symbols, the ancient clothes of Christians. They have been worn since the very earliest Church; therefore they represent the continuity of the Christian ministry and of the act which the Church performs when they are used. This is good symbolism which says something plain about God's action. In our time surely it is advisable that we should use this kind of symbolic interpretation rather than the other.

Certain symbolic actions are sacramental. They can be identified quite simply. A sacrament is a symbol which conveys what it represents. The symbol becomes an agent whereby something which is not purely imaginative is accomplished. Thus in Baptism we not only wash the child to represent the possibility of newness of life; Christ Himself by this act makes the child a member of the community of the cleansing. In the Eucharist the bread and the wine not only represent Christ; they actually are the means whereby He comes to us in communion. The number of sacraments is a mooted question. The relationship between the symbols and the reality which is conveyed has been the cause of vigorous debate and conflict in the Church. It would not be useful to discuss these problems here. The very important matter which we should recognize is the function of sacraments as a means of divine communication.

There is a doctrine which came to be known in the

Middle Ages as *ex opere operato* ("by virtue of the action"). This means that a sacrament is a direct instrument of God. It means that so long as the covenanted conditions are fulfilled, the divine event happens. In particular, it signifies that the character of the minister does not determine the effectiveness of his sacramental ministry. In times past this doctrine has often been taught in a very mechanical way which has brought it into disrepute. This is unfortunate because there is something deeply Christian and truly evangelical about it. It means that God reaches us by grace, not by our works. It means that He can enter our lives and communicate His redemption to us even below the level of conscious response.

This deals with several recurring problems. In certain traditions it has been customary teaching that when God forgives a man, he receives an emotional assurance of the fact. However, it is surely true that many people do not possess personalities capable of this reaction. In fact they may find themselves trying to induce such feelings and creating in themselves a false spiritual condition. Even worse, a repentant man may suffer from depression, and believe that God has not forgiven him. There is the other problem of not being able to respond emotionally to God's gifts, because of fatigue or illness, or even the near approach of death. In all of these situations, there is a liturgical remedy. Whether in the Holy Communion, in absolution, in unction, or in some other sacramental act, the Church gives the assurance that if we participate in the action faithfully, God reaches us, and does the work in us which has been appointed by His promises. Thus the guilty man is absolved then and there if he truly repents. The dying man is united with Christ through his communion. Such acts as these become vehicles of God's sovereign grace, of His creative Word.

All such liturgical, sacramental deeds must be interpreted very carefully lest they become formal. Obviously the state of mind and soul of the participant is utterly important. We can receive no sacramental benefit except by faith.

The two sacraments, Baptism and the Eucharist, commonly called the sacraments of the Gospel, are the pre-eminent liturgical means of receiving the Word of God. Both of them are currently subject to re-interpretation.

Within recent years there has been a movement to reform the understanding and practice of Holy Baptism. The Church has come more fully to appreciate this, the basic sacrament upon which all other sacraments depend. We have relearned its essentially corporate nature. We have stressed the necessity of proper preparation. We have recognized its proper completion in Confirmation. We have understood that a real future churchmanship is implied. Some clergy have doubted the propriety of baptizing infants when there is little probability of later participation in the life of the Church. This, of course, can never be certainly known. The validity of infant baptism must be maintained. What is conveyed in this sacrament is beyond human prediction, beyond consciousness.

It may seem that of all sacraments the one which would convey the least of the Word of God to the receiver would be Baptism. As we look upon the tiny child in the arms of the godparents, how, we may wonder, could such a being receive the Word of God? In fact, we may question the reality of the godparents taking the promises on behalf of the infant. Yet, this very sacrament forms the ground of all other later receiving of the Word. As soon as the infant becomes aware of religious reality at all, he knows that God has done something about him even before he knew His Name. All that he receives from God he receives in the context of his previous divine acceptance. Baptism is something which was *begun* in him at the font. It is the onset of a great power within his life.

We make a dreadful mistake when we regard Baptism as a completed act. It is an initiation, a beginning. At the moment of the washing, God claims the child as His own. He acknowledges His adoption of that child. He gives the child status in the family of God and the Kingdom of Heaven. This word is spoken through the sacramental act, and from that moment forth the child belongs within the fellowship of redemption. The child is reared in the confidence that he is already a Christian. He belongs to the Church, the Body of Christ, into which he is already incorporated. This awareness is the basis for normal Christian life. It gives the confidence of God's concern which opens the minds and hearts of men to His acts.

Christians rely too little on their Baptism. In moments of temptation and trial, they would do well to remember what God did for them in this sacrament. They would do well to say to themselves again and again as Luther did, "I have been baptized!"

Confirmation completes the initiation. The exact nature of the gift of the Spirit in that sacrament has never been adequately defined, nor can it be. In the early Church it followed immediately after Baptism. Naturally most of the converts were adults, so the double action of washing and the laying on of hands was accompanied by the confession of conscious faith. In the West, these two parts have been separated for practical reasons. This seems to us who accept this custom to be useful. The gift of the Spirit in Confirmation is a continuation of the gift in Baptism. It is for the same purpose as Baptism, that we may be able to live the Christian life as members of the Christian Church.

In this connection, something should be said about preparation for Baptism and for Confirmation. One of the plain reasons why so much churchmanship is nominal is that people have not been made ready for these sacraments. Technically, and of course, really, they have been initiated in the Church. However, they may have been sorely unprepared. This is a problem which naturally devolves upon the Christian ministry. It is also the responsibility of the laity. In particular the question of whether or not Holy Baptism has been fully appreciated and used by the child depends to a great extent upon the faithfulness of parents and godparents. When the latter are unbelieving, unpracticing persons, chosen as a social compliment, something rather close to blasphemy has occurred. Fortunately, the Church appears to be coming aware of the need to take these matters seriously.

The solemnity with which Baptism is administered is also a factor of grave importance. Cute little baptistries, remote from the congregation, may provide a cozy atmosphere for a family affair, but they are hardly appropriate places for initiation into the family of God. We should be thankful that public Baptism has been so widely revived. A further factor which needs attention is the actual use of water. So often this has degenerated into some very unimpressive action. It should be recalled that the Baptism in the New Testament was by total immersion. This was at least a vigorous action. No person who had been through it could possibly believe that nothing had happened. A time may come when it would be advisable to revive the custom. This is not now necessary or practical, but surely it should be clear in the way in which we baptize that the person receiving the sacrament is being washed. This is as important for the congregation as for the initiate. The Word of God in Baptism is received by the congregation as well as the initiate. It is an ever renewed declaration of God's relationship to them through Christ. One of the better developments of the Liturgical Movement is the renewal of Baptismal vows, especially at Easter. This custom should prevent a congregation from feeling that its Baptism is over and done.

The other sacrament of the Gospel, the Eucharist, is the central act of Christian worship. This fact is being recognized far and wide throughout Christendom, not only in the Catholic type of Churches but also in definitely Protestant areas. In fact, some of the most valuable Eucharistic theology is being written by Christians in the Reformation traditions.

The Eucharist is central not only because it is "the Lord's own service," the only form of regular worship which He instituted; nor yet simply because this is the sacrament of His actual presence. The Eucharist is central also because of its completeness. It has within its action all of the essential elements of Christian faith, including the Word of God.

The Word of God permeates the Eucharist. To perceive the true meaning of this act, we must ever return to its origin. The Church is greatly indebted to the re-examination of the New Testament sources by scholars within recent years. From their findings, particularly the work of Dom Gregory Dix, it has emerged that what Jesus was doing at the Last Supper was not instituting a new ceremonial meal, but re-interpreting an old one. That is to say, that from that moment when He said, "This is My Body and this is My Blood," He changed the meaning of the feast of the Old Covenant. He declared the future and final nature of this ritual eating and drinking of His disciples. The act which He thus did determined the significance of His death and therefore of His Resurrection.

This was Jesus speaking His own word about His own sacrifice. One element in the Eucharist, therefore, is, as St. Paul put it, "showing forth the Lord's death." Every time the Holy Communion is celebrated, therefore, the Word declares Himself again. The meaning of His death is made known. Recognizing that the Eucharist is a sort of acted sermon preached by Christ, does not deny the reality of the Real Presence. When Christians have a full Eucharistic belief, when they know, however they may define it, that Jesus Christ is present, exactly as He said He would be, under the forms of bread and wine, then the element of the Word is wonderfully vivid. It is Christ Himself at His own altar speaking the saving Word to His own. It is not so much that we are talking about Jesus in the Eucharist, it is rather that we hear Him speaking about Himself. This is a language of action. When the Word is spoken something happens.

There have been many theories of consecration. The debate as to the moment when the bread and wine become the Body and Blood of Christ, the question of how it happens—all such matters are legitimate subjects for theological discussion. They may not be capable of exact definition. It appears to be the original conception that the consecration occurs by prayer. Normally within this prayer there are the Words of Institution. During the Middle Ages they came to be considered the Words of Consecration. There is very good reason to object to an exclusive focus upon the Words of Institution as a formula of consecration. On the other hand they obviously play an important part in the making of the Eucharist what it is. They identify the act. They become Christ's own "Executory Word," as Romano Guardini has put it:

> Therefore when the priest utters the words, they are not merely reported, they rise and create. Obviously, at this point, we do not simply hear a man talking. The priest pronounces the words, certainly; but they are not his. He is only their bearer; and he does not bear them by reason of his personal faith or piety or moral strength, but by means of his office, through which he executes the Lord's directions. The true speaker remains Christ. He alone can speak thus.[1]

All of this sounds very much like the first chapter of Genesis and the prologue to the Fourth Gospel. The focus of attention in Eucharistic theology for centuries has been almost exclusively on the questions of the Real Presence and sacrifice. In fact in the minds of many people Eucharistic devotion is primarily a matter having to do with redemption and the forgiveness of sins. This has overemphasized the penitential element to the exclusion of the mood of thanksgiving. Perhaps a better balance could be restored as we sense that the Eucharist has to do with creation and re-creation. This is signified by the "Executory Word" of the Eucharist being said over the bread and wine. The function of the elements is understood in a proper theology of the Offertory.

[1] Romano Guardini, *Meditations before Mass*, trans. by E. C. Briefs (Westminster, Maryland: The Newman Press, 1956), p. 73.

The meaning of the Offertory has been recovered in the Church. There are doubtless some who still think of it only as the occasion for taking the collection, accompanied by the necessary preparations setting forth enough bread and enough wine to be used for the communion. Fortunately that is a passing misconception. The elements of bread and wine which were used in the ceremonial meal of the Old Covenant of the Hebrews and were therefore taken by Jesus into the Eucharist at the Last Supper have a great and obvious meaning. They symbolize our common life and the provision God has made for it in material things. When the offertory is made, we are presenting our lives to God under the forms of bread and wine— our bodies, our food, our work, our love, our human relationships. These are imperfect gifts. They need cleansing and transformation. This is part of the meaning of the Eucharist, that God gives His ruined creation back to us again through the action of His living Word, Jesus Christ, who in His Body and His Blood makes them new again. This is God's Word about His creation.

The ultimate purpose of the Eucharist is the gift of eternal life. The words of administration are a continual reminder of this fact—"preserve thy body and soul unto everlasting life." Unhappily there is not enough in most of our rites to express the eschatological element in the Eucharist. This is one of the essential aspects of the Holy Communion. Jesus at the Last Supper made this ever so clear when He said:

"Take, eat; this is my body." And he took a cup, and when he had given thanks he gave it to them, saying, "Drink of it, all of you; for this is my blood of the covenant, which is poured out for many for the forgiveness of sins. I tell you I shall not drink again of this fruit of the vine until that day when I drink it new with you in my Father's kingdom."
—*St. Matthew 26:26-29 RSV*

St. Paul in the earliest account of the institution concludes with the words "For as often as you eat this bread and drink the cup, you proclaim the Lord's death until he comes" (RSV). Surely one of the tasks of the Church in this age is to recover this eucharistic word of expectation of the coming of the Kingdom of God.

It would be impossible to detail all the ways in which the Word appears in the Eucharist because from one standpoint the Eucharist is created by the Word. When one understands the Word of God in the context of the Eucharist, he realizes that this is no mere verbal phenomenon. The Christian is in communion with the Word in a powerful re-creative action.

How can one prepare for such a tremendous experience? There still lingers in the minds of many people the strange notion that the Holy Communion is for worthy folk. Of course, the fact is exactly opposite. Jesus Christ came to save sinners. If we are to receive this Word, the requirement therefore is not fancied goodness but real repentance. The Church gives far too little guidance to people in this matter. Most of the forms for self-examination in little books of devotion are practically useless if not positively misleading. There is one recent exception. Pastor Max Thurian of the French Community of Taizé has prepared an excellent series of questions which can be found in his monograph *Confession*. Here are a few of his penetrating queries. These have to do with truth.

1. Have I failed in frankness or truth in speaking to my superiors, my friends, my wife, in order to avoid a punishment, a reproof, or the necessity of giving something up?

2. Do I tell lies in order to show off, or through vanity?

3. Am I often hypocritical, hiding my true thoughts or feelings from my neighbor in order to gain some advantage?

4. Do I love the truth, or do I allow myself to live "in the dark" through laziness, negligence or indifference?[2]

Such realistic self-examination should precede every Eucharist. It would give substance to the General

[2] Max Thurian, *Confession* (Studies in Ministry and Worship, G. W. H. Lampe, ed.) trans. by Edwin Hudson (Naperville, Illinois: Alec R. Allenson, Inc., 1958), p. 137.

Confession which leads to the Absolution. There are many people who do not realize the great gift in this sacramental act of forgiveness. It is a wonderful thing to realize that whether in public or in private, when one truly repents and unfeignedly believes, Christ then and there through His ministers bestows pardon and deliverance. This is one of the great ways in which the Word of God is given liturgically. There would be much less mental anguish and anxiety from guilt if Christians had a fuller sense of this great blessing, and we would be better able to receive the Eucharist.

There is more to preparing to receive the Word of God in the Eucharist than just penitence. We have to be open to the meaning of each particular celebration. This involves thorough familiarity beforehand with the prayers and lections of the day. It would be good to spend some time the night before in anticipation of the next day's Eucharist. The liturgical day begins in the evening, and "sleeping on" one's preparation is a very useful way of making it real. One can often appropriate what one has read and thought more profoundly if it is done before the night's rest.

The preparation should be made with a real awareness of the meaning of the Christian Year. The recurrence of the seasons is a tremendous device for receiving the Word of God. Quite obviously it has an important teaching value. As the various events of our salvation are celebrated in sequence, they become far more real to us. Even traditions that once prided themselves on rejecting the Church Year are gratefully restoring its use. There is drama and even pageantry in the recurring seasons, but the Christian Year is more than just a didactic device.

The Christian Year is an aspect of the Real Presence. When we have a sense of the divine action in the Eucharist, when we believe that Jesus Christ truly meets us at His altar, then the Christian festivals become more than memorials. At Christmas we speak of the Nativity as Christ's being born to us *today*. At Easter we greet each other with "He *is* Risen." We find ourselves joyfully participating in the saving acts of God. Frequently people remark that they wish they could have seen Jesus. Perhaps there is even some sense of injustice in the fact that we live at a time so many centuries from His—"I wish I had been with Him then." The Christian Year makes it possible for us to be with Him now. The Word is with His people, bestowing upon them the gifts which God gave in His mighty acts in history. The year of the Christian is a means of receiving Him.

When the truth of the awesome realities of the Eucharist is realized then inevitably there is a real participation in the celebration. Reverence is no problem for one who has a sense of the holy. The communicant does not let himself become bored in the sacramental presence of Christ because of the many people making their communions on a Sunday morning. Furthermore, the sense of the holy is a great stimulation to Christian inventiveness. There will be an ever increasing ingenuity to revive and develop ceremonial means to make clear the significance of the liturgical action. We now again have offertory processions and celebrations facing the people. All of these things help men to receive with greater realism.

There are two other liturgical functions which need to be understood more adequately as great opportunities for receiving the Word; namely, Holy Matrimony and the Burial of the Dead. In both instances the pressures of social custom obscure the proclamation. However, these are important moments of crisis in human life when not only those immediately involved but their friends and acquaintances are waiting for a word of some sort.

It is increasingly difficult to bear witness to the Christian doctrine of marriage. Yet in our Prayer Book service with its tremendous assertion of the indissolubility of marriage we have the opportunity to declare it again and again under the most impressive circumstances. It is incumbent upon the clergy that this should be done not only with beauty and dignity but also with very ample explanation beforehand. A neglected chance to do this is the wedding rehearsal which should surely contain a public explanation to the participants of the awesome meaning of the act in which they are about to be engaged.

In the Burial of the Dead we have the obligation of confronting the unchristian cult of the dead which now thrives among us. There have been many incisive criticisms of this dreadful development which has at its base nothing but pagan fear. Our funerals should be austere. Whenever possible they should be in the church. Surely there should be no compromise with the positively unchristian interest in the exhibition of the body. Here is the moment for the word of judgment and the word of Resurrection to be offered to people very conscious of their mortality though not so conscious of their sin. This is an evangelistic opportunity which the Church needs to exploit.

In spite of the discouragement Christians may feel in connection with marriages and funerals in our society, there is one real reason for satisfaction. The custom of celebrating the Holy Communion on these occasions is growing. This is, of course, the old Christian way, and it has an obvious appropriateness. When the Eucharist follows a wedding, it means that the first act of the bride and groom together is communion in Christ. This will never be forgotten by them. At a burial, in the midst of the suffering brought by loneliness, grief, and often shock, the sacrament not only presents an exhortation to trust in God, but actually brings real reunion with the dead through communion with the Risen Lord. Surely when the Holy Communion is provided on such occasions there can be no question of the Christian intent of the function. It is the greatest witness that can be borne to the Gospel in these human crises.

It may be well for us now to consider very explicitly the various ways in which we can receive the Word of God through the Scriptures in the liturgy. The Bible is read in church during the services in many ways. Here is the most obvious, though not necessarily the deepest, receiving of the Word.

It is a good thing when the place of reading in the church is made glorious. A great lectern with a massive Bible standing, perhaps, in the center of the choir speaks of the holiness of the Word. It is not necessary that we should preserve the convention of locating the reading desk on one side of the chancel facing the congregation as the Victorians taught us. Above all, it is not inevitable that the book should rest upon a spread eagle, the symbolism of which has never been quite clear. The most important thing about the place of reading is that it should be in a location from which the reader can be heard.

The manner of reading is also important. When the Bible is read in the congregation, this is a moment of real presence. This will be conveyed by the reader who senses the fact himself. He will not be hasty or unintelligible, but will set forth the passage with reverence and dignity. A great offence which is committed by the clergy is to attempt to make the lections so personal that the impression is given that they think they wrote the Bible themselves. The true reader conveys a sense of objectivity and "otherness" in this ministry.

The manner of hearing is as important as the manner of reading. Again Romano Guardini has some vivid comments on this matter; particularly about the habit of using prayer books in church:

> Solemn reading requires listening, not simultaneous reading. Otherwise why read aloud at all? Our bookish upbringing is to blame for this unnaturalness. Most deplorably, it encourages people to read when they should listen. As a result, the fairytale has died and poetry has lost its power; for its resonant, wise, fervent, and festive language is meant to be heard, not read. . . .
>
> Perhaps at this point someone may protest: "But these are mere esthetic details which matter very little.

The main thing is that the believers receive and understand the word of God—whether by reading or hearing is of no import." As a matter of fact, this question is vital. In silent reading that frail and powerful reality called "word" is incomplete.

It remains unfinished, entangled in print, corporal; vital parts are still lacking. The hurrying eye brings fleeting images to the imagination; the intelligence gains but a hazy "comprehension," and the result is of small worth. What has been lost belongs to the essence of the liturgical event. No longer does the sacred word unfold in its full spiritual-corporal reality and soar through space to the listener, to be heard and received into his life. Would it be a loss if men ceased to convey their most fervent thoughts in living speech, and instead communicated with each other only in writing? Definitely. All the bodily vitality of the ringing word would vanish. In the realm of faith also the loss would be shattering. After all, Christ Himself spoke of hearing. He never said: "He who has eyes to read, read!"[3]

Bible reading in the congregation is thus a very different thing from Bible reading alone. One can receive the Word with a greater sense of the reality of the encounter when he hears it in the Church. The living, spoken Word is a great power.

There are two main types of lections, the lessons for the Daily Offices, and the lessons for the Eucharist. In the Book of Common Prayer, these are the First and Second Lessons at Morning and Evening

[3] Guardini, *op. cit.*, pp. 11-12.

Prayer, and the Epistle and Gospel in the Order for the Holy Communion.

In the Daily Offices, the purpose of the lessons is manifold. Naturally they normally have to do with the season of the Church Year. They also give the opportunity for a selective and continuous reading of Holy Scripture. One of the values of a lectionary is that it indicates the Scripture which is pertinent to the season, and guides the congregation to consider it at the appropriate time.

The lessons at the Eucharist have a different aspect from the lessons at the Daily Offices because they are part of a different kind of action. In the daily forms of Morning and Evening Prayer there is more of a contemplative mood. In the Eucharist the congregation has gathered to do something. The first part of the service, the Ante-Communion or Pro-Anaphora, is clearly a preparation for something greater yet to come. There is a mood of expectancy. Yet it is the lessons which determine the content of that mood. The Eucharist of Advent is different from the Eucharist of Easter to a large extent because the lessons are different. How sad a thing it is that we have lost an Old Testament lesson from the Eucharist! When anyone has witnessed a celebration of the liturgy of the Church of South India, he realizes how much more complete the service is when both Testaments are read. Another excellence of that rite is the way in which the Scripture is announced: "Hear the Word of God as it is written. . . ." This is a great improvement on the feeble Prayer Book announcements "Here beginneth . . ." and "The Holy Gospel is written in. . . ."

The reading of the Epistle before the Gospel is a fortunate order. It indicates something which is commonly forgotten: namely, that contrary to their New Testament order, the Epistles were written before the Gospels. The Epistle generally requires considerable concentration. It is probably the passage of Scripture which is least understood. There may be need for revision of the liturgical Epistles for this very reason as well as the inadequacy of some of the selections. The bewilderment of most folk would be immediately dispelled if they simply read the Epistle beforehand with a simple commentary.

The Gospel is the most solemn reading of the Scripture in the liturgy. Very frequently a great opportunity is missed because of the absence of certain simple clear ceremonies. It was the custom of the early Church to have a special Gospel book, and to permit it to rest at all times upon the altar. Surely, it would be good to have a special book for this purpose, one that can be clearly seen by the whole congregation, no matter how large the church. The announcement of the Gospel is important. This should be solemnly done. The congregation, including the choir, might well turn to face the book. Before and after the Gospel the book can be shown to the people and perhaps elevated. These signs speak clearly of what comes to pass in this moment. In fact, they represent quite clearly the early Christian conception of the Church, the *ekklesia*, the community created by the Word.

So the fact emerges that in all our worship God's Word is there and we encounter it. The liturgy is a living dialogue in which we participate. This has been splendidly expressed by the French pastor and theologian J.-D. Benoit:

> This dialogue is communion. Behind the words of the dialogue there are living realities. God's Word is not mere discursive intellectual explanation intended to enlighten our minds; it is an act of God, a creative word, a sovereign *fiat*. It is a word which breaks, which overthrows, which lays hold on man and calls into being that which does not exist. God's Word is inseparable from his grace; for the soul which hears it, it is the gift of grace. In its full sense, the Word of God is God himself communicating himself and giving himself to us.
>
> Man's reply to God is also a living word, a word that expresses realities, a word which is a giving of ourselves, so that the dialogue of worship becomes an effective encounter by the community with God, the community

offering itself to God in its weakness and nakedness, and God coming to the community in self-giving power.[4]

---

[4] J.-D. Benoit, *Liturgical Renewal* (Studies in Ministry and Worship), (Naperville, Illinois: Alec R. Allenson, Inc., 1958), pp. 59-60.

CHAPTER IV

RECEIVING THE WORD OF GOD IN PREACHING

An AWESOME moment recurs in the life of a preacher. He stands before his congregation week by week and says, "In the Name of the Father, and of the Son, and of the Holy Ghost." They respond, "Amen," then sit down, and look up. Something is about to happen, something declared to be in the Name of God. Will it happen? The preacher knows that a meeting can take place through him between God and His people. He also knows that this meeting has occurred with powerful results in the most dissimilar situations throughout history. However, it does not always happen. Karl Barth, the great Swiss theologian and preacher, has provided a vivid description of this urgent moment:

> On Sunday morning when the bells ring to call the congregation and minister to church, there is in the air an *expectancy* that something great, crucial, and even

momentous is to *happen*. How strong this expectancy is in the people who are interested, or even whether there are any people whatever who consciously cherish it, is not our question now. Expectancy is inherent in the whole situation. . . .

Here is a *building*, old or new, of which the very architecture, even apart from the symbols, paintings, and appointments which adorn it, betrays the fact that it is thought of as a place of extraordinary doings. Here are *people*, only two or three, perhaps, as sometimes happens in this country, or perhaps even a few hundred, who, impelled by a strange instinct or will, stream toward this building, where they seek—*what*? Satisfaction of an old habit? But whence came this old habit? Entertainment and instruction? Very strange entertainment and instruction it is! Edification? So they say, but what is edification? Do they know? Do they really know at all why they are here? In any case here they are—even though they be shrunk in number to one little old woman—and their being here points to the event that is expected or appears to be expected, or at least, if the place be dead and deserted, was once expected here.

And here above all is a man, upon whom the expectation of the apparently imminent event seems to rest in a special way, not only because he has studied the technique of the event and is supposed to have mastered it, not only because he is paid and employed by the community or is tolerated almost without opposition in the function evidently associated with the event, but also because freedom is displayed here as well as law: the man himself chose this profession, God knows from what understanding or misunderstanding of it, and he has now for better or for worse wedded his short, his only life to the expectation of the event. . . .

And then the man will have the congregation *sing* ancient songs full of weighty and weird memories, strange ghostly witnesses of the sufferings, struggles, and triumphs of the long departed fathers, all leading to the edge of an immeasurable event, all, whether the minister and people understand what they are singing or not, full of reminiscences of God, always of God. "God is present!" God *is* present. The whole situation witnesses, cries, simply shouts of it, even when in minister or people there arises questioning, wretchedness, or despair. Then perhaps it is witnessed to best of all— better than when the real problem is obscured or concealed by abundant human success.[1]

Such a profound expectation of preaching contrasts sadly with the superficial way in which many persons regard it. If there is such a possibility in sermons, it is necessary that we understand what preaching really is.

A sermon is an event. It is only secondarily a composition. Clearly it is something which happens between people. A man speaks and they listen. The listening is just as important as the speaking. Our concern at this moment is to recognize that preaching is in the nature of personal encounter.

A sermon can happen only once. A sermon cannot

[1] Karl Barth, *The Word of God and the Word of Man*, trans. by Douglas Horton (New York: Torchbook ed., Harper & Brothers), pp. 104-107 *passim*.

be preached again, any more than a conversation can be held more than once. The words may be written and read exactly again and again, but each time it will be a different sermon because the situation has changed. Even if the preacher is the same and the people are the same, time has passed, and it is a new event because life has changed.

The uniqueness of the sermon may be the reason why sermons generally make such poor reading. In the nineteenth century there was a great vogue of printing sermons. Great series of volumes lie in parish and clerical libraries as a testimony to this fad. However elegant these works may be as literary compositions, still the moment of their preaching can never be recovered by the reader. They have become essays and no longer sermons. One can realize this vividly as he reads the accounts of the mysterious stillness of Newman's late afternoon sermons at the University Church in Oxford, or the thundering eloquence of Liddon to the great congregations under the dome of St. Paul's. Something happened in such times and places that can never belong to us as we simply read what they wrote. Because of the nature of preaching as personal encounter it might be well to suggest to many clergymen that they should consider more direct methods in preaching. Many a man in the pulpit has suddenly discovered the nature of his task when he has finally had the courage to do away with manuscript and even notes to look his congregation in the eye and to speak to them face to face.

The great encounter, however, is not between the preacher and the people. It is between God and the people. This is an essential understanding of a sermon which is often lacking because of the way in which the personality of the preacher may intrude. A certain Swedish bishop said that he had not used a sermon illustration for twenty years because he feared that too much of himself would stand between God and the congregation. The things which interested him might have too great a prominence. This is a rather extreme expedient, but his motive might well be apprehended by many who feel that the primary function of a sermon is to interest or even to entertain. When the preacher does assert his own individuality too vividly the reason may well be that the congregation has tempted him by their encouragement or even demand to make things personal. A preacher is in a perilous place because he stands before man for God. It is indeed an impossible position. There is no one worthy to preach, and no one who can preach worthily.

Sometimes it is said that sermons should come out of the experience of the preacher. Naturally he should know what he is talking about. Surely it can be expected that he should speak with conviction coming from real faith. However, there is a true sense in which the preacher should speak *beyond* his experience. Consider what his real position is when he must declare the judgment of God. He cannot do this as an innocent man speaking to the guilty. Nor can he limit his preaching to his practice. He is the first member of his own congregation. Time and again he must receive the Word of God from himself for his own need.

The situation of the preacher is like the situation of the priest when he must communicate himself. Sometimes members of the congregation say to the preacher, "You were speaking directly to me. How did you know?" All the time he was speaking directly to himself. There is a preposition which expresses this predicament. How much better it is to say that a sermon is preached *under* a text rather than *from* a text! The preacher must first receive the Word of God himself before he can declare it. When he stands before the Church, he stands also as a member of the Church, a sinful and mortal man having often to say with knowledge and concern things which pertain to his own need as well as the need of his congregation.

When this is understood, both by the preacher and the people, then the miracle in the situation appears. When men receive the Word of God it is more than the work of a good man. It is the power of God.

Sometimes the preacher learns that someone in the congregation has been truly converted or, perhaps, prevented from committing suicide. When this happens, a preacher has no right to claim that this was the result of his gifts. Such happenings are too tremendous for any man to take credit for them. A true preacher knows that it is in spite of himself, not because of himself, that the Word of God is effective.

Who is this man, the preacher? He is one who has been set apart. This has occurred because of something which happened in his own life. First he was "called." There is a strange conception abroad, even among instructed churchmen, about the nature of vocation. Often it is assumed that there must have been some moment when the voice of God almost audibly spoke to a young man desiring to know what he should do with his life. Sometimes indeed this sort of thing does happen. More often there is a struggle involving real bewilderment and questioning. Frequently vocation is a process lasting many years. One thing, however, is certain. There is always in a true vocation an element of natural protest. As we read the stories of the call of the prophets in the Old Testament, this is vividly expressed. It is not an entirely pleasant discovery to find that one must speak the Word of God. In typical reaction Jeremiah tries to avoid the issue by confessing his weakness "Ah, Lord God! behold, I

cannot speak: for I am a child." Christ Himself
struggled in temptation in the desert as God made
known to Him His call.

Those who know something of theological students
realize that there is always in a sensitive man offering
himself for Holy Orders some tendency toward
flight. In fact, it is a frequent experience for a man
to become quite terrified before his ordination. This
is, however, accompanied by the same kind of reassurance that came to the prophets classically expressed
in the words of Jeremiah, "Be not afraid of their faces:
for I am with thee to deliver thee, saith the Lord."
Though the burden be great, so also is the joy. When
a man realizes that he has been truly called, he also
knows that he has been given an awful privilege—
actually to speak in the Name of God.

This man, the preacher, was also ordained. The
Church has often recognized that there are Christians
not in the clergy who may have a special gift for
declaring the Word of God. These are sometimes permitted to preach, but this is the exception. The essential thing about the relationship between ordination
and preaching is that no man takes this ministry upon
himself. It is not sufficient to be sure of one's vocation.
One must also be sent by the Church. A man does not
stand before a congregation with the authority of his
own intellect, education, or eloquence, and surely not

his own goodness. The ordained preacher speaks by virtue of his commission given to him by the Church. When the congregation understands this, they are capable of receiving the Word more fully than when they think of the preacher only as an individual personality.

It is essential for the congregation to understand itself as well as the preacher. The same people in a theater or lecture hall would be a different reality. A congregation is not just an audience; it is part of the Church. In the New Testament the Church is understood as the company which has been gathered by the Word of God. The Greek word *ekklesia* which is used to designate the Church has within it the concept of the Christian congregation. In the original language the word means an assembly gathered by a herald to hear news. The Church is the congregation of those who have been called together by the Gospel of God. Whenever the Word of God is preached, it creates the congregation, and the response is as essential as the proclamation.

The congregation is not just a passive group of hearers. Any public speaker knows that his audience can play a decisive part in the effectiveness of his address. It is an obvious fact that a speaker develops an awareness of the attitude of those before him. An interested audience is inclined to be silent, with little restlessness, coughing, and movement. This gives as-

surance to the speaker and frees him for better utterance. This is naturally true in preaching as well as in
any other public speaking. Sometimes it is assumed
that a good audience is created by interesting speaking. It is equally true that good speaking can be created
by a good audience. The opposite is surely true. Anyone who has had the exasperating experience of trying to preach to a congregation in a compulsory chapel
service where the students practically defy the
preacher to interest them can understand the power
of the congregation on this simple, psychological level.

In a parish there is, however, a much more profound function for the congregation than alertness
to what is being said. The most important attitude
which makes possible a real sermon is expectancy. As
Karl Barth pointed out in the passage quoted above,
the very physical aspect of the church and the service
speaks of an anticipation of an important event. A
good congregation presents itself as though it knew
that something momentous is about to happen. It
knows what it has a right to expect in a sermon. In
fact, it makes a demand that what is said from the
pulpit should be a sermon.

It is the custom in courses on homiletics to have theological students criticize the sermons which their fellow students preach. In a certain course of this sort

the lecturer insisted that each student begin his comment by answering the question, "Is it a sermon?" This is the question which every congregation has a right to ask whenever it is confronted by words from the pulpit.

We can base a definition of a sermon on Jesus' own preaching.[2]

> And Jesus returned in the power of the Spirit into Galilee, and a report concerning him went out through all the surrounding country. And he taught in their synagogues, being glorified by all.
>
> And he came to Nazareth, where he had been brought up; and he went to the synagogue, as his custom was, on the sabbath day. And he stood up to read; and there was given to him the book of the prophet Isaiah. He opened the book and found the place where it was written,
>
>> "The Spirit of the Lord is upon me,
>> because he has anointed me to preach
>>   good news to the poor.
>> He has sent me to proclaim release
>>   to the captives
>> and recovering of sight to the blind,
>> to set at liberty those who are
>>   oppressed,
>> to proclaim the acceptable year of
>>   the Lord."

[2] I am indebted to Yngve Brilioth, the late Archbishop of Uppsala, for this suggestion made in his Donellan Lectures, *Landmarks in the History of Preaching* (London, S.P.C.K., 1950).

And he closed the book, and gave it back to the attendant, and sat down; and the eyes of all in the synagogue were fixed on him. And he began to say to them, "Today this scripture has been fulfilled in your hearing." And all spoke well of him, and wondered at the gracious words which proceeded out of his mouth; and they said, "Is not this Joseph's son?"

And he went down to Capernaum, a city of Galilee. And he was teaching them on the sabbath; and they were astonished at his teaching, for his word was with authority.

—St. Luke 4:14-32 RSV

From this account we can perceive that true preaching has three essential characteristics; it is an act of worship; it is scriptural; and it is apostolic.

1. *A sermon is an act of worship.* It is perfectly plain that there is much preaching which is properly outside of the confines of regular Church services. When Jesus preached His sermon in the synagogue, He was indeed in the context of the liturgy of His people. But He did preach in the field, on the hills, and by the sea. Wherever He went preaching, it was perfectly apparent that He was preaching not only before men but also before God. His words were a sacrificial self-offering, for it is because of His preaching that He was crucified. All that He said still fills men with a sense of the reality and presence of God. This is a characteristic of any true sermon. It need

not be eloquent, but it must be about God, and have
within it the awareness of His presence.

Many years ago the writer of this book heard a
preacher who had come from England read the Scripture and preach a sermon which was a turning point
in his life. There was something new in this man's
manner. There was an awe and humility in his utterance which were so plain that the feeling they invoked
is still a vivid memory. The sermon was not eloquent but it made its great impact because the preacher
knew that he was engaged in an act of worship with
the congregation before the living God. This is hard
to forget.

One of the great detractions from this element in
preaching is the self-assertion of the preacher. Some
preachers have been great pulpit personalities. Their
churches have been called by their names rather than
by the name of their dedications. A man of eloquence
can enlighten, entertain, and even amuse the congregation. He may gather great throngs. He may become
a celebrity. He may influence the course of the
Church's life. Though he has great power, he still may
not be preaching. The fatal defect of what he says
from the pulpit is that it is not an act of worship.

For many years there has been a school of thought
which has considered preaching to be conveying
truth through personality. There is some validity in

this notion, but there is great danger of its leading a man and a congregation to overemphasize individuality. This is symbolically dealt with in the wisdom of liturgical Churches in seeing to it that the preacher is vested. In fact, the purpose of the robes, quite contrary to what is sometimes thought, is not to emphasize a man's ego, but to suppress it. In this connection, is there not good ground now for restoring the old use of the black gown for preaching? The use of Eucharistic vestments is widely accepted at the present time because it represents the dictinctiveness of the Eucharistic act. There is an equal distinctiveness about the act of preaching in Christian worship. In some places a preaching gown as well as Eucharistic vestments is employed to make this point plain.

2. *A sermon is scriptural.* When Jesus declared His mission, he expounded a passage from the Prophecy of Isaiah in the Old Testament. It is normal for preachers to use texts. Indeed, it has to be said that many times the text is about all there is in the sermon that is scriptural. Great Christian preaching has always been from the Bible. Many times it is very definitely expository or exegetical. These forms of preaching are by no means outmoded. It is a consistent complaint of laymen that they do not know the Bible and that the preacher does not use it.

One of the best types of preaching would surely

be the direct explanation of what some of the most profound books in the Bible declare. Consider for instance the powerful effect in history which has been exercised by St. Paul's Epistle to the Romans. This book was the basis of the earthshaking events of the Reformation. John Wesley was converted hearing Luther's preface to the epistle. The great theological revival on the continent of Europe in our own century began with Barth's commentary on the same book, written to express a more profound understanding of man's predicament during the time of the First World War. Surely there is an ever present need for the exposition of such a book!

Biblical preaching is, however, not only preaching about the Bible. A sermon needs to be expressed in the great thought forms of the Scriptures as well as using their content. It is the interpretation of the scriptural point of view, not simply, as it were, quotations from the book.

There is a kind of preaching which extols the Bible but is not really Biblical. It claims its authority from the Bible. The constant cry of the preacher is, "The Bible says. . . ." Sometimes the preacher actually carries a Bible in his hand all the time that he is preaching. However, the whole mood of this sort of utterance may be wrong. It appears that the Bible is being trusted rather than God. Great passages of Scripture may be quoted from the King James Version, but the effect is unreal. When the Bible is considered a miraculous book, there is always the lurking suspicion in the minds of alert and intelligent folk that this use of it is really contrary to known truth.

Biblical preaching should be preaching of the whole Bible. A true sermon (apart from special occasions) should be related to the Church's seasons. One of the most fortunate aspects of the liturgical Church is the possession of a lectionary for the Christian Year. In the Church of Sweden, there is a system whereby the texts for the sermons are chosen officially and published for three-year periods. Most churchmen would find this a rather confining requirement. However, a lectionary is a great guide to Biblical preaching. It helps the preacher to preach the whole Word of God, and it also guides the congregation in its expectation of what will be heard on Sunday morning.

It also helps the preacher in another way. One of the most rewarding experiences that a clergyman may have is to be forced to interpret an uncongenial passage from the Bible. In the process of preparation, his own scriptural knowledge becomes fuller. Many a time he makes the rewarding discovery that there is something there which he never knew. Faithfulness to a lectionary is fairness to the congregation. Surely there are occasions when it is right to depart from it, but when such departure is known to be the exception, preaching is actually enriched. The people are delivered from the special tastes and spiritual provinciality of the preacher.

There are certain great occasions when the congregation and the preacher have a special sense of the immediacy of the Word. One of the most notable of these is the so-called Three Hour Service, or the Preaching of the Passion. This began rather recently in the history of preaching, being a seventeenth-century Jesuit development in South America. It has now gained great acceptance throughout the whole of Christendom. Recently it has incurred a great deal of criticism, particularly from those who have liturgical interests. It is perfectly true that the Three Hours is not the great service of Good Friday, but it is also true that the people come. It is a very grave decision to abolish a custom by which so much can be accomplished. There have been certain schemes of combining the liturgy with meditations so that the whole of the offices for Good Friday are observed during this time. Something, however, is lost when this is done. When a congregation for three hours presents itself to hear the Word of God from the lips of Christ on Calvary, there is a great opportunity for real Biblical preaching. One of the strangest and most wonderful discoveries which can be made on Good Friday is the inexhaustibility of the Word of God. Over a decade of preaching the Three Hour services, this writer would bear witness that there is ever something new to be declared about the Seven Last Words. The congregation at such a moment may well feel that it is actually present on Calvary. "Were you there when they crucified our Lord?" is answered, "Yes."

3. *A sermon is apostolic.* It is common to call good preaching "prophetic." Something of the assurance of the prophets is certainly required in the Christian pulpit. Furthermore, there is the ever-present need for relating the Word of God to contemporary affairs, which was the vocation of the prophets. However, the term "apostolic" in its true sense may be more adequate to describe the Christian sermon.

As Frederick Denison Maurice pointed out, the prophetic element in Hebrew religion has been taken up and fulfilled by Jesus and transformed by Him into an apostolic ministry. The mood of the prophet and the mood of the apostle are somewhat different. The prophet lives in expectation. So, also, does the apostle. But the apostle lives in the expectation of something he has already seen. He has been sent forth from an event which has already come to pass.

This, of course, is one of the meanings of ordination. The prophet is sent to a special situation, a particular need in a particular time, and in meeting that need he may feel compelled to do extraordinary things and may even have ecstatic experiences. With the apostle, there is more ordinariness in his method. He is one who must be prepared to speak in all times and in all places. But he must have the same kind of authority with which the prophet spoke. He must be able to say with assurance, "Thus saith the Lord."

A congregation has a right to expect to receive an authoritative utterance from the pulpit. In the synagogue of Nazareth, Jesus startled His hearers by the assurance with which He spoke. "Is this not Joseph's son?" they asked. Others reported that He could be distinguished from the scribes and Pharisees because He taught with authority.

Some years ago a visitor from England to our shores returned to write an article on American religion. He said that our preaching could be summarized in the phrase, "May I suggest that you try to be good?"[3] It is not certain that the same expression might not be applied in his own native land as well, because for years there has been a tentativeness about preaching in the Anglo-Saxon world except in the provinces of fundamentalism. Part of this is due to somewhat theological reasons. It has frequently been said, for instance, that the Anglican communion has an Augustinian Prayer Book but a Pelagian pulpit. This may no longer be

[3] A. R. Vidler, "The Appalling Religiousness of America," *Theology*, January, 1948, Vol. LI, No. 331, p. 45.

fair. Surely there was a period, at least before the last war, when the prevalent liberalism in Anglo-Saxon religion made preaching tend to moralistic homilies. Sometimes there was in it a deep sense of the importance of Christian ethics, both individually and socially. Sometimes there was an honest repudiation of a former doctrinaire dogmatism that made religion irrelevant to life. Whatever the reasons, the result produced was in strong contrast to the preaching of the New Testament and the greatest Christians in any age.

Recently the word *kerygma* has come into prominence in Church circles. This is the New Testament term for preaching. It means a proclamation. It could never mean simply exhortation or the giving of good advice. The proclamation is of the Gospel, which as we have all known from our Sunday School days means the Good News. If utterances from pulpits can by no stretch of the imagination be described as proclaiming the Good News from God, then clearly they are not sermons, but something else, however estimable.

This naturally leads to a question of the propriety of the so-called teaching sermon. Is there not a real question whether this is not almost a contradiction in terms? Naturally there will be information and instruction in any proclamation of the Gospel, but the mood of true teaching, the mood of the classroom, is in contrast to the mood of the Church. There is an urgency and an immediacy about preaching which is not necessary to teaching.

A distinction needs to be made between authority and authoritarianism. It is possible for a self-assertive, even a fanatical, person to claim that he speaks with authority because he declares himself emphatically. This is, of course, foolishness, though it is an ever present temptation for the clergy. The true authority which appears in preaching is the authority of the conclusive Act of God in Jesus Christ. It is the proclamation of the tremendous reversal of sin, pain, and destruction through the death and Resurrection of Jesus Christ.

It is impossible to preach the resurrection of the dead and the coming of the Kingdom of God in a tentative way. A congregation should, therefore, expect to receive the Word of God as under authority. This does not mean that they must subject their minds to another man's intelligence and will. No one has lordship over their faith. It does mean that they have a right to expect from the preacher assurance and clearness so that there can be no doubt about the faith wherein they stand together.

Herein lies a great responsibility of the laity to make possible the freedom of the pulpit and the right of the preacher to speak with authority. The events

of the Gospel must be related to the affairs of the
world. The preacher must be able to present the implications of God's revelation in direct terms. Jesus
did it and was crucified for it. There are warnings in
the New Testament that Christians can expect the
same sort of reaction if they follow His example.
Surely this treatment should not come from within
the Church. When it does, it is generally in the form
of a criticism of the parson for mixing politics or
economics with religion. The preacher has no right
to use his apostolic authority outside of the apostolic
realm. That is to say, he is not ordained to preach
economics or politics, but he is ordained to declare
the relationship between the Word of God and the
ways of men.

A new device has recently been developed to show
the relationship between the Word of God and ordinary problems. This is called "the dialogue sermon."
Several persons participate in it, each taking his own
part representing various elements in the divine and
human situation. This has been a useful form of
religious drama. But again the question may be raised
whether or not it is really preaching. There is an in-
directness about it which does not seem consistent
with the proclamation of the Gospel. Furthermore,
there is the inevitable question whether or not the
objections to the Christian faith, inasmuch as they

are invented by believers, may not be straw men easily knocked down. This is a temporary form of Christian expression, which doubtless has its place, but cannot be accepted as adequate preaching.

If a sermon is to be apostolic, it must obviously depend on the Holy Spirit. The apostolate was created by the Pentecostal experience. The preaching of the early Church was never thought by the first Christians to have been effective because of its cleverness. St. Paul finds a scandal in Christian preaching. He writes to the Church in Corinth: "For the preaching of the cross is to them that perish foolishness; but unto us which are saved it is the power of God." Again he wrote: "It pleased God by the foolishness of preaching to save them that believe."

St. Paul recognized that receiving the Gospel is not the result of good argument. People do not fail to be Christians because they are unintelligent. Here is a mystery beyond our understanding, but there is light in it. The Apostles knew that the response to their preaching was a result of the work of the Holy Spirit in their hearers. This continues to be true. The preacher must keep ever within him an awareness that God is present in the congregation to use his sermon for the fulfillment of His purpose. A good sermon in composition and delivery frequently fails when a poorer one makes a difference. The preacher never knows why, but it may be that when he is in the pulpit he is not alone with the congregation.

The congregation, then, has a right to expect a sermon to be an act of worship, scriptural, and apostolic. When this expectation is regularly fulfilled, the congregation can come with a deep anticipation of a momentous meeting with God. Therefore, it is obvious that the disparagement of preaching is a serious matter. Unhappily, there has been much of it. Sometimes it has been motivated by the clergy who do not care for preparation and delivery of sermons. It is also the work of those who make a false alternative between the liturgy and the Word of God. In a Church with a Prayer Book, it is fortunate that the clergy cannot deprive the congregation totally of the Gospel, but without the proclamation of the living relationship between God and His people in the present, the liturgy is not enough.

Several other forms of resistance to preaching exist. Inattention in the congregation creates a real problem. With our present vivid means of mass communication people require more stimulation to arrest their attention than in former times. Of course there are some who simply say they do not like sermons and refuse to listen. Others will listen to only a certain type of preaching. Perhaps they get used to their own pastor and can hear his style only. Maybe if the preacher reads, the people are irritated.

Commonly the problem is the length of a sermon. How long should a sermon be? A common dogma is that the Word of God is twenty minutes long. It is impossible to make uniform demands in the matter of time. There are certain subjects that cannot be treated in twenty minutes, others that can be vividly presented in ten. In the last analysis, whether one resists the Word of God is determined within the human heart. When the importance of the sermon is understood, it will be heard.

Naturally there are poor preachers. These are not necessarily men with poor voices, poor grammar, or poor learning. Some of the greatest preachers have been men who violated all the rules of homiletics. They have had handicaps as public speakers. These men made their impact because they were able to convey their concern for the Gospel with vividness. The really poor preacher is the one who does not care. What do we do when we find ourselves confronted by him? It is probable that there will be something that he says which is true. In fact, our desperation to discover it may make it more effective. It is likely that he will use something of the Bible, and this also we can hear. Beyond that he may have a function to create within us, in our exasperation, some apprehension of what he has not said. God can disclose Himself in contrast to that man.

Preparation for hearing the Word of God is as important as preparation for the sacraments. There is a general preparation which is essential. As in the case of any encounter with God, we must be ready with faith. It was said even of Jesus that in some places He could not do His works because of the unbelief of the people. This means first that we must approach a sermon with trust in God. We must expect that He wills to reach us with His truth. Real open-heartedness involves willingness to hear what may hurt. The preacher must give warning and minister judgment, must speak of sin and death as well as of love and life. Faith will accept this fact. A preacher is not a salesman. It is his duty to persuade, but not necessarily to please.

Faith is, however, more than an attitude; it must be informed. One hears of other days when the laity knew Scripture and doctrine. Sometimes they were the terror of the preacher. Few are the preachers who fear their people on these grounds any more. A lack of Biblical knowledge, ignorance of Christian teaching and history on the part of congregations, keeps much preaching infantile. Many a sermon cannot be heard because it is "over people's heads." This would not be so if men were of greater stature as Christians.

There is also a need for immediate preparation. It is important that we should approach the Church having a clear knowledge of what we can expect to hear. We need to know the season and its meaning, the lections of the day. What a serious matter it is if people are taken by surprise because of their own laziness! The clergy can sometimes help by announcing sermon subjects carefully worded.

Reading the Church page on a Saturday in a metropolitan newspaper is a shocking experience. Displayed again and again are subjects for Sunday sermons which are deliberately calculated to entice an audience. Sometimes the inducement is mystification, sometimes even vulgarity. There are certain subjects such as commentaries on current events which can be calculated to get a hearing. In reaction to all this, many a preacher has decided in disgust not to publish sermon topics at all. Though his motive is righteous (we assume it is not laziness), he has missed the opportunity of revealing what sort of religion he professes and also of giving guidance to the people who must prepare to hear him.

The time has come for a real rediscovery of the nature of preaching. Many people have been returning to their churches, curious about religion. Radio and television have reached still others with the Gospel. The question is asked whether these media will eventually supersede churchgoing. Certainly they cannot give the sacramental life of Christians to the world with its necessity of physical meeting. Neither can they really take the place of the preaching of the Word. There needs to be a congregation as well as a preacher. When the cleric on television stares into a battery of lamps and cameras, that is a vastly different situation from the one he finds in church. There is no response except ratings and the mail. The immediacy is all gone and he stands remote and alone. Surely this cannot be the future answer!

Finally, a plea for Evangelical Catholicism! The place where the rediscovery of preaching will be most fully made is where the great historic sacramental tradition of the Church is found and accepted. We have seen before how the Word of God can be received in the liturgy. When this is done and it is accompanied by a real reception of the Word of God in preaching, the Church becomes strong and men are prepared to face the world. Let us recover the use of the word *Evangelical*, not as the antithesis to *Catholic*, but as the strong positive assertion of the things which belong to the Gospel of God.

There have been great moments in the life of the Church in history when the Church has been able to save the affairs of men and nations. We are living in one of the most dangerous periods of history. Our very existence as a species is threatened. Millions have no religion and have actually turned to vicious but powerful philosophies. All of this we know; it makes us hourly anxious. Surely this is no time for the Church to keep silence! Surely this is a time to hear the Word of God!

THE WORD OF GOD
IN THE CHRISTIAN

And he said to me, "Son of man, eat what is offered
to you; eat this scroll, and go, speak to the house of
Israel." So I opened my mouth, and he gave me the scroll
to eat. And he said to me, "Son of man, eat this scroll
that I give you and fill your stomach with it." Then I
ate it; and it was in my mouth as sweet as honey.

And he said to me, "Son of man, go, get you to the
house of Israel, and speak with my words to them. For
you are not sent to a people of foreign speech and a
hard language, but to the house of Israel—not to many
peoples of foreign speech and a hard language, whose
words you cannot understand. Surely, if I sent you to
such, they would listen to you. But the house of Israel
will not listen to you; for they are not willing to listen
to me; because all the house of Israel are of a hard forehead and of a stubborn heart. Behold, I have made your
face hard against their faces, and your forehead hard
against their foreheads. Like adamant harder than flint
have I made your forehead; fear them not, nor be dis-
mayed at their looks, for they are a rebellious house."
Moreover he said to me, "Son of man, all my words that

I shall speak to you receive in your heart, and hear with
your ears. And go, get you to the exiles, to your people,
and say to them, 'Thus says the Lord God'; whether
they hear or refuse to hear."

—*Ezekiel 3:1-11 RSV*

When the Word truly comes to the Christian, it
becomes a part of him. This union is profound, of a
sort which inevitably calls for the metaphor of eating.
In this strange passage from the call of Ezekiel, the
prophet is commanded to devour the scroll. In the
Gospel according to St. John there are similar utterances. In one ever memorable discourse, Jesus is portrayed as saying:

"Truly, truly, I say to you, he who believes has eternal life. I am the bread of life. Your fathers ate the
manna in the wilderness, and they died. This is the bread
which comes down from heaven, that a man may eat of
it and not die. I am the living bread which came down
from heaven; if any one eats of this bread, he will live
for ever; and the bread which I shall give for the life
of the world is my flesh."

The Jews then disputed among themselves, saying,
"How can this man give us his flesh to eat?" So Jesus
said to them, "Truly, truly, I say to you, unless you eat
the flesh of the Son of man and drink his blood, you
have no life in you; he who eats my flesh and drinks my
blood has eternal life, and I will raise him up at the last
day. For my flesh is food indeed, and my blood is drink
indeed. He who eats my flesh and drinks my blood
abides in me, and I in him. As the living Father sent me,

and I live because of the Father, so he who eats me will live because of me. This is the bread which came down from heaven, not such as the fathers ate and died; he who eats this bread will live for ever." This he said in the synagogue, as he taught at Capernaum.
— *St. John 6:47-59 RSV*

Christians have disputed for centuries whether these words refer to the teaching of Jesus, which is to be received into their lives, or whether this is a Eucharistic reference having to do with the actual reception of communion. This is an unnecessary and false alternative. Receiving the Word of God, whether in the Bible and preaching or in the liturgy in its various forms, is receiving Jesus Christ. When He comes into a man's life, His advent is no casual thing. It means the real penetration of his whole being. It is an act which can be expressed only in the language of union; Christ in us and we in Christ. This is obviously not just an individual matter. Each of us in our union with Christ naturally becomes united to each other. This is God's plan for the re-creation and restoration of our race through His living Word.

As we face the problem of meaninglessness with the Word of God, we discover that what the Christian faith has to offer is not just an intellectual answer. It must be insisted, however, that part of the answer is intellectual. There is no place in Christian practice for the really irrational. When this has been said, it must be recognized that the Christian answer in the Word of God simply will not provide the kind of satisfaction some are seeking. It will not be accepted by those who want merely a sense of spiritual security. Certainly it will not be wanted by those who wish to use religion solely for the solution of their problems, psychic or physical. When the Word of God enters into a Christian, there is a consequent transformation:

> But to all who received him, who believed in his name, he gave power to become children of God; who were born, not of blood nor of the will of the flesh nor of the will of man, but of God.
>
> —*St. John 1:12-13 RSV*

We have not only this observation of the Evangelist, but the evidence of the lives of Christ's disciples through the centuries to show that great changes have occurred in those who have shared this experience. The certainty which comes to the Christian comes through his involvement in this relationship. It is the by-product of his willing discipleship, and not available to those who are unprepared for two costly experiences: conversion and witness.

Conversion happens to those who receive the Word of God. In these days of popular revivalism it is important to make plain that this does not necessarily involve a sudden, overwhelming emotion. There are, indeed, times in life when God gives men a strong and immediate sense that He is dealing with them. Whether this happens or not, there can still be conversion. In fact, Baptism, the very beginning of Christian life, implies conversion, and is the ground of it. By it, we become members of the community in which this transformation takes place. In each of the stages of Christian growth, there is some change in the shape of our lives. Conversion should be thought of as a process, as a perpetual revolution whereby we keep turning away from our self-centeredness to God-centeredness.

The work of the Word of God in conversion is to produce this wonderful change by keeping before us and within us the real truth about God's nature and our relation to Him. The Word also gives us the power to overcome our natural human rebelliousness, and in this we have available to us the strength of Him by whom all things were made.

Conversion involves repentance, which is not simply remorse, but the continual return to God as we learn more and more of Him and therefore of our sin. But it is more than repentance; it is the remaking of life. In the present time when we are so much aware of the formative influences of early years, with our adulation of youth, we may tend to think that change is possible only for the young. This is a tremendous mistake. The Christian faith teaches that the possibility of conversion exists until the very hour of death, and the final purpose of conversion is fulfilled at that very moment when the sons of God enter into eternal life.

Witness is also inevitable to those who receive the Word of God. It is a consequence of conversion. This responsibility is difficult for the casual Christian. He is afraid and embarrassed to speak about his faith. There is a sense of indecency about religious conversation. Some of this may be the result of a proper sense of propriety. Indeed, pious, unctuous talk is unpleasant. However, this is not true Christian witness. When the Word of God is really in a Christian, he cannot keep it to himself.

In our society, it is becoming increasingly unpopular to take a stand. People are afraid of controversial issues. There is no question about it: the Word of God *is* controversial. We are warned in the Bible that we can expect a conflict between the Gospel and the world. We are warned that being disciples of Jesus means taking up a cross. This does not always happen in a dramatic way, but the risk is always there. When a man is willing to take this risk, and openly to confess, by his actions as well as his conversation, that he is a believer, he can become the most effective exponent of the faith. In this connection the laity have a greater evangelistic power than the clergy, because their motives are not suspected.

Christian witness is of many sorts. There is the basic confession of faith which involves the knowledge of the Word of God in its fullness. A man should always be able to explain what he believes, and to have his explanation make sense.

Furthermore, it is incumbent upon anyone whose life has been converted to be willing to tell what God has done for him. There is altogether too little of this kind of expression. It must be done with common sense as well as enthusiasm, but there are many times when such a personal word would have compelling conviction.

Finally, there is the very difficult kind of witness in the realm of moral decisions, individual and corporate. Every man in the place where he finds his vocation must make ethical judgments. These in the long run determine what he is. These judgments are never absolutely pure, but they can be governed by a strong sense of God's Word which will make a man willing to sacrifice. The real question about Christian practice is not determined by the amount of work a man does around the church, but the way in which his family, his business, his recreations, and his intellectual life reveal the marks of Christian decision.

The Church now faces the responsibility of confronting a new age. There is a work of Christian witness which cannot be done by individuals in their individuality. We are passing through a revolution equal in dimension to the fall of Rome, the Renaissance, and the Industrial Revolution. We are tremendously awed by the prospect of the conquest of space, but there are other aspects of the change in our culture which are equally important. When we consider the development of psychiatry, the extraordinary medical advances, prospects of automation, the power of mass communications, and when we dare to realize that all of this takes place under the threat of catastrophic extinction—we can truly believe that there never was an age which needed the Word of God more critically. It is the task of the Church to bear witness toward these great developments, to interpret their meaning and to seek their control for the benefit of men. This is a tremendous task and it can never be done by a Church which is unwilling to spend itself totally.

Christian witness always involves the willingness to give one's life. The martyrs of the Church may seem very far away from us. They belong to other ages and other lands. We do not seem to be called on to bear witness unto death, although others now are doing so. In some ways our predicament is more difficult because the issues are not clear. But we can never be sure that the day may not come when obedience to the Word of God may not involve a total oblation. More Christians have lost their lives for their faith in this generation than in any other since Christ. Many of those who have died as martyrs would, in the earlier days of their life, have felt as safe as we do. It is a good thing to contemplate this matter from time to time. When a man is ready for such a possibility, he is certainly sure and secure. There is no meaninglessness in that life.

Receiving the Word of God is the most important experience in life. As it comes to us in its promised ways, as we truly accept its coming, every present moment of our life has meaning. We experience now by faith what we shall know by sight when we shall meet Him face to face.